MW00461236

MERGING LIVES

by

G. Turcin

DORRANCE
PUBLISHING CO
EST. 1920
PITTSBURGH, PENNSYLVANIA 15238

Dorrance Publishing Co
585 Alpha Drive
Pittsburgh, PA 15238
Visit our website at *www.dorrancebookstore.com*

ISBN: 978-1-6376-4309-9
eISBN: 978-1-6376-4623-6

Progress and changes are happening with all aspects of our lives. Some are drastic, representing a landmark achievement; some are more subtle and elusive in perception, but nevertheless important in the process of progress and change.

In this story book I seek to provide a basic insight and understanding of a simple man and his wife striving for the better. The story as it unfolds is bittersweet, reflecting trying times, leaving the country of birth for a better place, leaving family and friends behind, and facing the unknown while believing that all will end well. It is intended to remind our daughter and her children of their roots, of a culture and a country they know very little about, and most of all: to let them know that life was not easy in the pursuit of happiness we found in America, and that the sacrifices made were well worth it.

When we were weak, disappointed, scared, and faced with what seemed insurmountable challenges, God seemed to have stepped in to carry us, to show us the ray of light that would renew our hopes and put us back on track. For this we would ever be grateful, and believe that everything in our lives happens for a reason.

ABOUT THE COUNTRY OF ROMANIA

The beginning of the national history of Romania can be set at the beginning of the 2nd century. The Roman Empire with its insatiable desire to conquer territories and amass natural resources, stationed their Legions in the territory of Dacia. By the end of the 3rd century, the Romans left behind a partly Christianized Daco-Roman population that was continuously exposed to the invasions of the migrating barbarian tribes. As a result, the Romanian nation is the product of the union between Romans and Dacians.

The characteristics of feudalism became essential during the 13th and 14th centuries with the establishment of the Romanian Principalities (self-governed territories) of Moldavia in the north and Wallachia in the south.

During this time the Principalities were unstable, without the infrastructure necessary to stop the Turkish continuous attempted invasions. In the 15th century the Turkish suzerainty took control of the Principalities and exploited them for the next 400 years.

At the beginning of the 18th century, the disastrous Phanariot (Greeks) phase began. The peasantry was ruthlessly exploited, brought to the brink of disaster. By having to pay increasingly high tributes, the peasants had to resort to desperate measures, such as burning their houses and fleeing the country to avoid payments. The only positive aspect of the Phanariot era was an elaborate cultured life. This influenced many young intellectual leaders to start travelling and staying abroad, mainly in France.

The national independence over Turks and Phanariots was established in 1877, when the characteristics of modern Romania started shaping up. With German capital, King Carol the 1st (1866-1914) built important industries, constructed railroads and established economic institutions. Carol the 2nd (1914-1940) continued the pro-French orientation, which formed the basis of Romanian policy. In 1940 under great pressure for political association with the Fascist regime, Romania lost Basarabia territory to Russia and parts of Transylvania to Hungary. The loss of these territories forced Carol the 2nd to abdicate the throne in favor of his son, Michael. In August 1944, in a last minute decision, King Michael joined the Allies and overthrew the Antonescu fascist regime.

The communist takeover began in 1947, December 30th, when King Michael abdicated from power and the Romanian People's Republic was established. Under the constitution of 1965, the Romanian People's Republic became the Socialist Republic of Romania.

The country continued to remain a communist country until 1989, when people of Romania revolted against president Ceausescu who brought the country to the brink of economic disaster. Nicolae Ceausescu and his wife Elena were arrested and given a speedy trial that resulted in a death conviction. The sentence was carried out on Christmas Eve 1989 when both the president and his wife were shot dead by the firing squad.

Major changes followed, and not necessarily better. The people of Romania wanted so badly the long overdue democracy, however, not being equipped for such a drastic change, the country entered a chaotic stage. The leaders elected came from the ones that were serving in the executive cabinet of the Communist party; the weak industry became even more fragmented with major mining exploitations closing their operations; disproportionate balance between the work force and the retired people; bribery and nepotism remained at its highest; the agriculture production managed through the communist collectives stopped producing and the land was divided and privatized; extremely high unemployment rate with people doing menial jobs throughout Europe; the health care subsidized by the government is almost nonexistent with sick people being sent home to die when they can't afford to pay for the medical supplies; and some longing after the communist regime that at least resembled some stability.

Romania, through its origin is a Latin country, located in the southern part of Europe. It covers an area of 91,700 square miles and has a population of about 20 million people. The density is approximately 250 people per square mile. The largest minority group is the Hungarian (9%) followed by the German group (3%). The other ethnic groups are the Serbs, Czechs and Slovaks, Russians, Tatars, and Romas.

My hometown

The settlement of Moldova Noua, my birthplace, came to be as a fusion between two settlements: Bosneak and Baron, back at the beginning of 1900. In 1968, due to its strong copper mining industry, it became one of the most important towns in the county of Caras-Severin, Romania. Growing up in the '50s, we still used the name Bosneak for the town, and Baron for the street we lived on.

At an altitude of 800 feet, on the north the town borders the skirts of the nearby mountains with peaks reaching 6,000 feet, and on the south the river Danube forms the natural border with Serbia. There are a string of dependent villages on the east and the west side. The roads connecting the villages were primitive, initially accommodating the horse pulled wagons that were the main way of transportation for goods and people. Later on, with population growth and the developing auto industry, the roads were improved a great deal accommodating the new demand.

The entire region is viewed by historians as one of the most important mining projects during the Roman empire. This industry resumed under the reign of Austro Hungarians and continued under the nationalization of the country when it became the Republic of Socialist Romania in 1965. The mining industry collapsed after the Revolution in 1989 when the country became democratic and the government lost control of the nationalized resources.

From 1965 the population of Moldova Noua grew constantly, reaching 14,000 by 2008. By nationalities there are 81% Romanians; 14% Serbs; 2% Romi (gipsy); 1% Hungarians; and 2% other nationalities combined. By religion, there are: 88.5% Orthodox; 4.5% Baptist; 4% Roman-Catholic; 2% Pentecostal; and 1.1% other.

The climate of Moldova Noua is continental-moderate with strong influences of sub-Mediterranean climate, characteristic to the 45 degrees north latitude. The four seasons are very distinct: The spring brings an abundance of lush green vegetation with broad leaves trees; the summers are hot but not humid; the fall dots the surroundings with beautiful colors of leaves; and the winter usually brings lots of snow with strong winds around the Danube channel. During the winter, most people lived in homes that were not equipped with an appropriate ventilation system and as a result they "smelled the wind" meaning that the wood stoves were choked by the strong wind, with the smoke going throughout the house. Our home was not equipped with a ventilation system and there are times that I can still "smell the wind", as this was a very unpleasant experience growing up. By the western standard of civilization, a home is built with a central heating/cooling system connected by air ducts. With no such systems available and affordable to common people, we created an air draft by opening windows and doors in the opposing sides of the house. It worked most of the time, trading comfort for necessity. Experiences like this lead to humbleness.

The tilt of our planet brought seasonal changes to our life, as it happens everywhere else in this world. In our corner of the world, we grew up enjoying four very distinct seasons. Perhaps in the urban areas, the seasonal changes were not perceived at the same depth as in the rural areas where we lived.

The spring brought a new impetus to get things ready for the year, agricultural or otherwise. It was like the entire community woke up from the winter hibernation. One could see more and more people around the yard, assessing the winter damage to the properties, picking up debris left from the windstorms, leaves, and broken tree branches. This was followed by tending the gardens tilling, seeding, and doing other improvement around the households as needed. With the temperature climbing up, there was less need to use firewood for heating the house, and the heavy winter clothes got stored away.

The summer days were longer and filled with other types of work that led to the upcoming harvest time: from keeping up with the gardens, safeguarding the fruit tree crops from uninvited guests, to tending for animals to produce for the next season's preserving plans.

In the fall, all were scurried in the haste of getting things done and in place before the rain and cold days came. The fields of grass were cut and the hay stored for winter animal use and insolation of the attics, the fruits were picked and canned, the firewood was gathered and stashed, the cheese was made, the sauerkraut was barreled, and the pigs got fattened.

From here, it was not long until the old man winter came, bringing lots of snow that seemed to have transformed the geography of the land with a festive scenery for the winter holidays. Before the winter holidays, almost all households butchered a fattened pig that would provide meat sustenance up to the next spring season.

And every year, more or less, the same seasonal cycle continued.

First Years of My Life

I was born in my grandparents' modest home on October 6, 1952 and I was the fourth child born to Ilie Turcin a Ranger, and his wife Elena a housewife. The oldest brother Gheorghe, died of unknown causes when he was two years old. My brother Ion is four years my senior, and my sister Maria, is two years older than me. I suppose my parents missed their first born so much that I was given the same name six years later, when I was born. We all lived in the same old little home with my grandparents, Gheorghe and Maria Gruescu, a retired coal miner and a housewife.

Times were hard for our family, as for the rest of the community we lived in. The financial sustenance for the family came from my dad's modest salary and grandfather's pension. This was supplemented by mom and grandma working a little vegetable garden, and raising some sheep and a cow. What could have been preserved for winter by the means of canning, salting, and smoking, it was, and helped a great deal. While we have heard of refrigeration, these kinds of appliances were something we have never had in our household in my first ten years of my life.

By the Western civilization standard of living, we were well below the poverty level. However, in our small little world with no base of comparison, we grew up happy, us children played outside all day no matter what season it was, without worries or concerns. In those days children had very few toys, rubber balls mainly, and small flashlights when they behaved and there was money left to buy them. We got our first store bought shoes when we started school at seven years of age.

Do not have a detailed recollection of the first five years of my life. Perhaps that has to do with writing about it after I turned sixty years old. However, there were some things that I will always remember: the image of the old little home with two small rooms and a cooking area; the entryway that was opened and functioned as a makeshift patio where we had our meals and washed up in a big square tin container; the square table and seven stools; and the dirt floors. This living area was built above a cellar where the family kept what was needed to be stored for a longer term through the winter. We had to climb about twelve steps to the patio and access the living area. Oftentimes some of us children would rock our little stools and fall off the stairs. My sister Maria still has a scar on her forehead from such a fall.

The home was located on the odd numbered side of the road (#313), over a creek that kept flowing year round, with an old wooden bridge over it. Quite a few years later, we replaced the wooden bridge with cement reinforced beams. What a difference it made, not only to the esthetics, but to the safety for all.

The yard was large enough (about a half acre) for an old barn for the one cow and sheep, the pig's pen, a vegetable garden, a chicken coop, the dog house, and the ever needed latrine. It should be obvious that no one had indoor plumbing in the area we lived in those days, nor did we have electricity. The drinking water was brought into the house with "the water bucket" from a well built on the neighbor's property, across the street. The "water bucket" had a small, enameled cup next to it on the stool, and used by all when drinking. My grandparents also had additional land scattered at different locations, for hay and fruit trees that were mainly walnuts, apples and plums.

We were for the most part self-sufficient and happy. And that's where our family of seven lived during my first six years of my life. Some of my life experiences will be difficult to understand, mainly because aside from my wife Elena (Neli) and Cristina up to five and a half years of age, none of you had similar experiences or struggles growing up. The first six years of my life, as described above, can't be elaborated further mainly because I don't remember much. However, as I moved through life growing up and interacting with others in different places, I continued to learn.

FIRST MOVE

Beginnings always bring us challenges, or at least that's the general perception among adults. For children on the other hand, they are a joy, a new way to discover the world, learn, and have fun.

When I was about five years old, my dad got a new job as a lumber yard manager, I believe still under the Forestry Department he worked as a Ranger. The lumber yard was located about ten miles from my grandparents' home to the west, between the villages of Susca and Pojejena, and about 700 yards north of the Danube river. In the north it neighbors the village of Radimna, populated mainly by Serbs. It was this entire region that had thick forests and a thriving lumber industry. The wood was cut and split at a yard length and transported down to the lumber yard via a wooden flume. The flume was running along Radimna creek that fed it with water at its highest point in the hills. It was something new for us kids to see and admire as it was one of the very few flumes in the Region. The most fun we had was when the flume got clogged and the workers swarmed around the area to unclog it to resume the normal flow. At the lower end there was a basin from where the wood was picked up manually by the working men and arranged nicely in stacks within the lumber yard.

From the lumber yard, the wood was taken with horse pulled wagons to the shore of the Danube, where the long barges were waiting to be loaded up and took the wood to further destinations: either down east toward the Black Sea, or up west toward Serbia. Oftentimes waiting to be loaded, the barge's sailors would come to shore and give us kids candies and some toys and get from us eggs and some other produce from the garden. We were happy to get what was given to us at the time, not really understanding the barter system.

The house we lived in belonged to the Forestry Department, and was to be used by the lumber yard manager and his family. With two spacious rooms and a kitchen, it was by far a better living arrangement than the grandparents' home, however, no indoor plumbing, but with electricity. In the entry area there was a telephone (crank inducer) that was to be used for lumber yard business. So, unlike many kids my age in 1957, I knew what a telephone was although I could not call any friends or relatives as they would not have one.

Next to the house on the west side, there was a small building with a grocery store intended to supply goods for the lumber yard workers and the nearby villagers. As kids, we were regular customers for candies and other goodies. On the east side, divided by a wooden fence there was a winery supplied by the nearby grape fields. I instantly took a liking to this establishment, fascinated by the winemaking equipment and the fermentation process in the huge barrels where the grapes were stomped on by people with bare feet. My favorite part was eating all kinds of grapes and drinking grape juice from my own plastic cup that I would carry in my pocket. We were allowed to roam the winery premises the way we felt like, as my grandfather who came to visit quite often, cooked for the Vintner and my dad supplied them with firewood. Little I knew then, that half a century later I would be the Vintner of my own winery, at the other end of the world.

The vegetable garden my mom had was perhaps three times bigger than the one at grandparents' house and oftentimes we kids were summoned to help work it. There were a few apricot trees, always loaded with fruits and we would nail blankets on the tree branches, lying leisurely on them. It was a perfect arrangement: store next door, winery on the other side of the property, plenty of fun with the flume, toys from the sailors, and endless ways to have fun.

Between the road in front of our house and the shore of the Danube, there was a strip of about 300 yards of clay deposits washed ashore by the large river. The people from the nearby villages would dig in and get the clay, mix it with straw and form it in wood forms to make bricks. It was interesting to see the big stacks of dried mud blocks set on fire and turning into red bricks. Primitive process, intensive labor, but profitable for poor people and their sustenance. One year the Danube flooded its banks, filling up the clay holes, with the water coming almost to the road in front of our house. When the water retrieved to the normal level, to our amazement the holes had fish left behind, mainly carp, still swimming and gasping for water. It was then that we would load them in the wheelbarrow and take them home. I really don't remember how our parents cooked or preserved the fish by salting and drying, however, I do remember it was a great deal of fun.

Those days, there were not many cars on the road, just some trucks and occasionally Russian made all-terrain vehicles, the equivalent of the American Jeep. The roads were not paved and crushed rock was occasionally thrown on it to stabilize the weather erosion. My dad had a bike and us kids would take it and self learned how to ride it. Many knee scrapes, but we learned how to do it, and never forgot.

FIRST TWO YEARS OF SCHOOL

I started school at seven, in the small village of Susca. Walked to school every day with my sister Maria, who was in the third grade. We would walk the mile long walk and have fun horsing around. I did like school and made friends with a couple of kids that I remained friends with all the way through adulthood, Stefan and Mircea. They would come to our house and we would play together having endless fun. The classes were combined: first grade with third, and second with fourth. This arrangement was very popular in the rural areas for the elementary schools, with not that many children enrolled. We had wood desks with a sitting bench, with the desks having an ink hole for the nib pens and calligraphy nibs used in the higher grades.

Our mom had a fourth grade education but knew how to read and write and was our tutor at home. We had time dedicated to homework, and she always ensured we did it. She was a devoted Baptist and would take us to the little church in Susca, every Sunday morning and evening. Until later on in life, my dad did not care much about this spiritual aspect of life.

It was about this time in my life when I had seen the first movie. It was in the nearby village of Pojejena and was projected by a movie caravan. The name was *Footprints in the Snow*, a Russian black and white made film that scared me a great deal when I saw a train locomotive coming toward me. This scene stays with me and I don't think I will ever forget it. The rest of the movie, I don't remember.

Besides the winery next door to our home, with the heavenly good grapes and juice, there were the black mulberry trees alongside the road. These trees produce such sweet fruits resembling the blackberries that we have in our backyard. The side effect: when kids eat these fruits that are sweet and very juicy, the clothes get stained, the teeth, the mouth, and that was not a pretty sight. But we were happy. Some of the work we did involved picking the leaves of the mulberry trees for the silkworms our parents grew on a contract with the government. I don't remember the entire process but I do recall bunk beds type, where we had silkworms laying and eating the leaves until they entered the cocoon stage. It was an additional income for the family and a lot of fun for us children.

In the back of our home, there were endless fields of beets planted by the "Collective". The Collective was a government sponsored organization, with people's individual lands taken by the government and worked by the entire community, with the mechanical equipment provided by the government. The produce went to the government for further distribution/sale, with a small share going to those that were enlisted in the Collective and worked the land. The harvested beets followed the same venue as the lumber: They were further transported by the barges either up the Danube, or down to the Black Sea. As people were paid very little for their work in the Collective or the lumber industry, theft was prevalent. There were watchmen at the Collective and the lumber yard to deter the thieves. I remember an occurrence when my dad confronted a watchman at the lumber yard when he was found asleep on the job. His explanation: "I was thinking about all my troubles Mr. Turcin." And nothing followed that.

Quite a few years down the road, after the revolution of 1989, there were many people that would have liked to maintain the "collective" system. After so many years, people forgot that their private lands were nationalized, got used to this system, and another change would bring more challenges to deal with. After the revolution, the land had to be divided again among owners, that oftentimes lived no longer in the country. Records were lost and the arguments about who owned what piece of land, became an ongoing debate.

14

MOVING BACK HOME

By the time I was ready to start the third grade, we moved back home with our grandparents who started the building of a new home for us all. It was fascinating to be part of this project at this early age and I am sure there were many things I did not understand about the process, however, many aspects of it came back to me when we would build our own home in the USA in 1992. The excitement about building a new home and the cost involved, were perhaps the only similarities found. The new home was built with rocks and bricks using mortar, and had a red tile roof. With three spacious rooms in the front and big windows, it was night to day kind of comparison to the old home. Each of the rooms had a wood stove but no ventilation system as we know it here in the USA. Quite a few years down the road, after we left Romania, our parents updated the wood stoves with Terra-cotta stoves. These were more efficient in producing heat and adequate direct exhaust outside through the stove pipes. There was electricity but no indoor plumbing, nor air duct ventilation system. Behind the three front rooms there was a long hallway from the entry door to the storage room at the end, about twenty-seven feet. The attic was used to store hay for the animals during the winter months and also worked as a good insulator for the house. There was an offsite kitchen, used for preparing and most of the time consuming the meals. Next to the kitchen our family had a water well that was about fifteen feet deep. It had a nice cover with a roof and functioning wheel system/bucket for getting the water. Us children became experts at turning the wheel and getting the water bucket up. Was much nicer than having to go across the street and carry the bucket full of water. Remember as it was yesterday: The water was cold, fresh, and when I got older we cooled our beer in the bucket of water that was lowered to the water level. Small progress, but nevertheless progress.

Continued going to finish elementary school (third and fourth grades) at a makeshift school located by the nearby mining area called "Floribunda" about a mile from our home. Again, the classes were mixed (first with third, and second with fourth). Remember doing well in school, was a "pioneer", the youngest adherent to a socialist system, and before finishing the fourth grade, was elected the Unit Leader, carrying the sign on my left arm of our school uniform. At the time, I was so proud of it. In retrospect, it's interesting how our stages of development in the society we live affects our mind sets. Direct correlation at first, until one starts learning different ways of life from people living in different places. With me, the disagreement started with reading about people and places, continuing my education and later on moving away, living life independently the best I could.

Life moved on at the same speed, very much uneventful. We would go to school, enjoy playing times, and when on school vacations and weekends we would take turns at taking the neighborhood sheep to the pasture. This was a day-long event that we would not mind, except that we had to get up early, round up the sheep from the neighborhood and take through the woods to the pasture area, a few miles away. The days were lost with not much to do, we would take naps, build fires, fry bacon and onions, drink water from the mountain springs, and dream. At the end of the day, we would take the flock of sheep back to the corral (stina) for the milking. There were a number of women (part of families working this arrangement) that were doing the milking and taking turns in getting the milk share for cheese making, etc. All of this was possible in our small neighborhood (about twenty households) only because people got along with their neighbors and respecting the elders was a must. The youngsters will never address the older folks by their first name. Those days will never be forgotten.

Our neighborhood of about twenty households was at the end of the street called the Baron, stretching for about two miles from downtown Moldova Noua (Bosneak), to where we lived. For me and other children, it was the center of the world, as we did not travel out of our area for more than ten miles, by that age. My close friends all had nicknames and were within one year of each other's age. Of my age was Capatina (big head), a distant cousin, a good hearted guy that liked to embellish things/stories.

One year younger, we had Danet (family nickname) who always wanted to have fun on someone else's account. He grew up to become a witty guy and died when he was fifty-six years old. He was also a distant cousin who had a younger sister. Then we had Chiftea, (his face resembled a flattened meatball) who was of a darker complexion and of course we did not miss the chance to rub in the gipsy allusion most of the time. He was a wise crack also and had a younger sister that as I grew older, started liking her very much. Last, there was Peroiu (exaggerated way of saying his family name). He was a year older but not always included in our small circle, mainly because his family was labeled by the neighborhood as not being very clean people. He grew up, had a family of four and just after he retired at fifty-five, died in a freak accident: While gathering firewood, a heavy branch came loose and hit him in the head, killing him instantly. My nickname was Dundu, named after my grandfather's nickname. I always enjoyed an informal leadership position in the group and I always attributed this to reading a lot and utilizing by far a more extensive vocabulary than the rest of my friends. From what I know, only Capatina and Chiftea are still alive, living their lives with their families in the same area where we grew up together.

We hardly had any store bought toys (perhaps a simple flashlight and rubber balls) but were very creative with making up games. We chased steel circles with a wire drive, we took our parents' bikes for rides, and in the winter we were sledding on the street that had about 2 percent incline. In the summer, older and younger children in the neighborhood got together and built a small dam across the creek that ran alongside our street. We built it a little ways up where the creek bed was a little wider and good for swimming. Rocks and sod held together and harnessed a pool of water that was about five feet deep. In the center, at the bottom there was a small gate (no bigger than a foot and a half square) that would go in and out according to filling or emptying the pool. For many years this was the highlight of our lost summers and that's how many of us learned to swim. It was always fun watching the water gush out through the gate when the pool got emptied. I remember one time, when taking off the gate a smaller kid neighbor got in and I pushed him under, not realizing that the water current could pin him across the gate opening and the kid would drown. The kid did not drown and somehow made it through the gate opening to the other side rolling with the gushing water. Bruised and hardly breathing he made it alive but I was scared out of my mind realizing that I could have killed him. The kid's name was Petrica, my next door younger neighbor who grew up, got married and had two small children, and when he was about thirty, died electrocuted while trying to steal some copper wire (live) from the nearby mine. It was embedded in the belief of many Romanians that stealing from the government was not the same as stealing from another person. In a Socialistic society, stealing from the government carried an aggravated level, as the social system was in charge of taking care of its people. Also, the false premise that it is okay to steal from the government, leads people to other societal evils: bribery, nepotism and corruption, to list a few. Regrettably, these societal evils continue to proliferate to these days, developing into a Gordian knot. Who knows, if in the distant or near future some Alexander or some new form of government will undo it, or end up cutting the knot.

We played soccer, card games, chess, backgammon, and the evenings were reserved for hide and seek. With an abundance of lightning bugs in our region, we enhanced the evening play by smearing the fluorescent part of the bug on our foreheads. Inspired by our ancestors' history, we played games with swords and shields, teaming against each other as Romans and Dacians. Our parents had a hard time finding us for the meal times and it was like pulling teeth when we had to go home at night. My childhood was happy and looking in retrospect, I would not trade those years for anything in the world.

Living a simple non sophisticated life, with limited resources and away from the evils of modern society, we were content with what we had. Without a base of comparison of a better life, we did not miss the benefits a better life would bring and at the same time, we were sheltered from its evils (i.e., drugs, parent defiance/rebelliousness, homelessness, etc.). With that said, we did not grow up to experience any serious traumatic lifestyle side effects, as our life was a simple one.

After quite a few years since defecting from the country, when going back to visit and meeting with old childhood friends, we all agreed that "we had the best of childhood life a child could have". I hope Cristina will say that we did the best we could with raising her.

GROWING UP IN THE '60S IN ROMANIA

Lagging behind quite a few years with the region's stage of development, many of the people born and living there, died before having an opportunity to see the rest of Romania. The part of the country we lived in (Moldova Nouă) was connected to the rest of the country by a highway not very well kept and unpaved (at the time), to Oravita located at about twenty miles northeast crossing a low mountain range (Piatra Alba). There was some rudimental bus shuttle system that made people sick with the poor ventilation, not very warm in the winter and very hot during summer days. In Oravita there was the nearest train station making the connection to the rest of the country, and those days travel by train was widely utilized by everyone as the roads were in such bad shape.

In the south, later on, the Port of Danube was built. The main purpose was for loading big ships and barges with wood, mineral products from the local mines, and agricultural produce, needed to be shipped down to the Black Sea or north to other European countries. There was also a watercraft (Salupa) providing people transportation to Orsova, about sixty miles east on Danube for train connections to the rest of the country. In the late '60s a road was built from Moldova Noua to Orsova, winding along the Danube river, dangerously narrow and curvy with the imminent risk of falling rocks from the abrupt slopes of the rocky hills. The roads connecting the neighboring villages/settlements were all unpaved and kept up with crushed rock for erosion stability. Those days one could see mainly delivery and logging trucks and some busses on the roads. On the other hand, there were

19

quite a few horse pulled wagons, used from personal transportation to hay and log hauling, moving market animals and supplies to the Saturday's public markets. At the public market (a very important day for all) people would buy feed (corn and grain), wheat and flower, animals, chickens, etc. The cost was never fixed, people would bargain prices with much bragging at the end of the day about the best prices some got. In 2006 when I went back home for a visit, there were still some horse pulled wagons on the road, however, most had car tires instead of the traditional hard wagon wheel. In that area of the country and other remote ones in the rest of the country, people were still using horses for plowing their fields.

In the spring most of us children enjoyed picking up the early snowdrops and later the fresh lilacs, from the nearby hills and taking them home to our parents. In a home with no ventilation system, the fresh smell of spring flowers made everyone happy. This was just about the time we no longer had to build the fire for heating the home, so the smell of smoke was soon forgotten. Not much happened in the spring besides cleaning the yard and getting the gardens ready for the new crop. We all worked at tilling the soil and mom and grandma would take care of the planting. Until the harvest, from this point on we were expected to water the garden daily by hauling the creek water with buckets, easy enough to do.

As Easter holiday came close, the entire neighborhood was getting ready for the lamb sacrifice. Almost every household would have at least a lamb butchered and ready for consumption at Easter. The traditional meal for the Easter holiday would start with a soup made of lamb, baked lamb leg or the entire side with baked potatoes and lettuce salad. It was a feast that we only enjoyed on a few occasions around Easter. My grandfather would be called by most everyone in the neighborhood for this task, and I was always on his toe so to speak, watching and learning the trade. Many years later after moving to America, I resumed this custom and was somewhat surprised to see some of my new friends joining me. We enjoyed the summer days, there was no school to worry about, plenty of things to do outside, especially swimming in our own neighborhood swimming pool.

Toward the end of the summer, after Dad cut the hay with his scythe, the women would help take bundles of hay on their back to the home's storage areas. At our home, we help put it in the attic for further use in the months ahead. Harvest in the produce from the gardens followed, with potatoes, onions and carrots all being stored on dry beds for use later on in the winter months. At this time also, the cheese got salted and preserved in the cheese barrel and the sauerkraut made in its barrel for further use in the months ahead. The firewood was cut and stacked, ready to use in the winter months, the only heating source.

Getting ready for winter took some planning ahead but people had it down pat as this was part of what they did every year. Again, I was by my grandfather's side admiring his work from killing the pig with a long sharp knife that went straight to the heart then to the throat, for bleeding out the blood. Next, cleaning the carcass to the point that there was no hair left with the skin shaved and totally clean. Then, the prep work for making thin and thick sausages (using the small and the large pig's casings), hams, bacon and salting the meat for the curing process. The fat was sorted out, used later for making soap. The meat was not cut as we are accustomed to see it here then wrapped, as we did not have refrigeration to preserve it. The hams, the sides, ribs were all separated, cured in salt then smoked for keeping and consuming throughout the winter months. For a longer keep, cured meat, bacon and sausages were fried and kept in a container covered with lard, so the air would not get to the meat and spoil it. Usually this would last until about Easter time. Not much from the sacrificed animal was thrown away, the dogs and cats were happy to get some scraps and the children always liked to kick around the inflated bladder until it popped. I will always remember how the pork smell changed during the process, from the repulsive offending smell at first, to the aromatic smell of cooked pork with a hint of garlic in it. The butchering process always ended with a large meal of fried pork with cornbread and sauerkraut, for those that did the work or were invited, a meal that I would not miss for anything in the world. I suppose this had a strong impact on me since as an adult I ended up taking up the trade my grandfather's way after we got established in the USA: making my own sausages, bacon, ham, etc. Some of my new friends here participated quite often at doing this with me and I think this will continue for as long as I can do it. While this is not a contemporary American household custom, it is dear to me.

The Christmas season stays in my memory through two things: the Christmas tree and the Christmas carols. The tree was always cut fresh from the nearby forest, not very difficult to get and bringing in a new fresh smell to the entire home. It was kept in the "good room", a room used only for guests and off limits to all the children. The tree decorations were simple, some homemade ornaments and sweet candies wrapped in aluminum foil of many colors. Times were hard and the candies could not be replaced every year, only when they started disappearing, and that usually happens when us children sneaked in the room, got the candy and left the wrapper hanging on the tree. After the church service, on Christmas eve we all gather around and our parents would light up the tree sparkles hanging on the branches. We all were mesmerized by the lit up tree and the symbol it stood for.

The Christmas carols time was also special because it involved some exciting prep time: finding the right bag with the shoulder strap (usually made by mom or Grandmother) to carry what we were given and bring home. The carol selection followed and what household to go to first. It did not take us long to figure out who the generous people were in our neighborhood. Usually children went around the neighborhood in age groups singing carols and getting whole walnuts, crackers, oranges and apples, and homemade pastries. We had a great time, bragging at home about "our loot". For Christmas presents we all got some candies carefully placed by Santa in our boots, left in the hallway impeccably clean and polished. We did not get much but we did not expect much either, and all of us were happy with whatever we got. Never really heard about the Children's Christmas list to Santa but we learned that rather fast when we got to America. Christmas was one of the major winter holidays celebrated at the Baptist church our family belonged to. Increased number of worship services, dressing up for the event, and the celebratory mood of all, brought great joy to those attending the services.

The New Year celebration followed. In religious households like ours, we were expected to go to the late church services worshiping together the New Year's arrival. Although late by the time we got back home, we would still find time to have some cold cuts of meat and bread for a midnight snack. The alcohol consumption was not sanctioned by the church, so we did not have any.

The other group of households (mainly Orthodox), not necessarily observing our Baptist religious customs, would go to a neighborhood gathering (usually held at the nearby elementary school), for listening to music, drinking, and playing games of cards. Nevertheless, the scope was the same: welcoming the New Year.

Probably this was one of the early lessons I got on the diversity of people's customs, religion related. Growing up I didn't see any of this, because I was shielded from it. Religious diversity wasn't considered a good thing in my home. I was taught that only our religion was right and the others should only be tolerated. By the age of eighteen, this close mindedness never sat well with me, therefore I did not want to get baptized in this religion. Later, I found myself distancing from the ecclesiastical life, and learning the realities of life on my own. In our journey to America, I have learned about other people's acceptance of us, with most showing kindness because it's what their faith taught them. And this learning continued with our submerging in the American culture, where the right to worship the way people choose is an individual right of all. No matter how many places I lived in after leaving Romania, no matter how many languages I learned, and no matter how many customs I was submerged in, the living heritage I grew up with, had and will always have a definite print on my life.

LIFE MOVES ON: MIDDLE SCHOOL

We were very happy in our corner of the world, enjoying what we had and living a life without any base of comparison to something else. As I grew up and getting ready to start middle school, it felt like getting close to a window: getting a clearer view of the world I lived in. Some incomprehensible changes came into my life and I did not do too well in accepting them. First came the new school structure: starting with the fifth grade, we had a different teacher for every subject making me feel not well engaged with them but rather disconnected. These feelings were the opposite of what I felt toward the elementary school teachers (one at each school I attended). Then, with the new environment came new friends, and not always of a positive influence. It was a struggle to finish the fifth grade and with such poor performance and behavior problems, I came close to being held back. Those days, the troublemakers had their heads shaved, a hairstyle I got used to having. At the assembly each school day before classes started, one would have no problem identifying who the troublemakers were. With puberty in the mix, I tried very hard to identify myself and make sense of all the new feelings I started experiencing, with no one guiding me through this. Things got better as I moved through the sixth and seventh grades. Looking back, I put the change in better on the account of starting to like reading even more. We had a well-stocked library in town and I became a voracious reader of everything I got my hands on, started to learn more about the world, other people's lives, different places and cultures and my mind opened up. As a result, my vocabulary expanded a great deal and was sought quite often by other children.

Departed Lives of Loved Ones and Funerals

It was just about when I turned fifteen years old when my beloved grandfather got sick by developing thrombosis and had to have his right leg amputated above his knee. Soon after the surgery, we found out that his leg was thrown in the garbage bin that held all refuse created by the hospital. As a teenager, learning about the realities of life, this was very confusing to me while the rest was the "reality of life" there. He did not take the new situation well and shortly after, he passed away at the age of seventy. I felt the entire world crumble under me when I lost my role model and mentor. I always felt closer to him than to anyone else in the family. My dad seems to have never been around for me those days because of his work, and Grandfather filled his absence in a great way. I will always remember this with fondness and one time visiting the old house, after emigrating to the U.S., I got his old miner's lamp. I had it refurbished and when looking at it I remember the good times growing up around him. Also, whenever I went back home to visit, I made sure I said hello to him at the cemetery.

Those days when the person died at home or at the hospital, the funeral process with the burial of the departed was entirely handled by the family and the community. The deceased was soon washed in a large wooden container, if not owned by the family it was borrowed from others, with women exclusively handling this task. Then the body was carefully lotioned with whatever was available to emanate a pleasant smell, the facial hair shaved and the fingernails trimmed. Then the body was clothed with the best new clothes available, usually older people would have the burial cloths, garments, shoes, put aside for when they were needed. The body of the departed would be taken on the table of the best room in the house for a couple days of viewing and further transferred to the upcoming casket. Friends, acquaintances, neighborhood people, church members, would come and go sharing positive things remembered from the departed's life. While this happened at the house, some workers were contracted to dig up the grave for returning the body to earth. As devoted Baptists, my grandparents had a family plot at the Baptist cemetery, located about a mile from our home on a neighboring hill. Don't know why, but I went to the cemetery with the couple of people hired to dig the grave on the same plot where my brother Gheorghe was buried about twenty some years before. His little coffin was rotten but still kept its shape and when the diggers removed the lid, his little skeleton was laid in it, resembling the contour of his little body. I will never forget the site of this encounter as it was very impactful, to actually be able to see the remains of my brother I shared the same name with while he died six years before I was born. With this discovery, my grandfather's grave was dug a bit deeper for my brother's remains to be reburied in the same grave. The pastor of the church would officiate a service at home with the choir songs and prayers said. This would follow with another church service by the graveside. The burial of the deceased was always accompanied by lamentations and wails, heard from afar. The number of people attending the funeral process at home and at the graveside was directly correlated to the popularity of the departed, true everywhere. In Romania, the funeral process for the deceased varied as dictated by the existing religious beliefs and regional customs, and continues the same way. Most people who knew the deceased would walk behind the horse pulled Hirsh to the grave side. Others would come in front of the house, watching in silence as the funeral procession went by. A similar process was followed when my grandmother passed, and continued with my dad and mom's passing, years later.

Moving forward about seven years since my mother passed, in 2020 we lost our beloved nephew Alin to complications of his pancreas. In a matter of a week's time he fell very ill with major abdominal pain and had to have an emergency surgery. He did not make it through the intensive recovery and was pronounced dead shortly after. He was forty-eight years old, and my sister's oldest son. The societal changes happening throughout the world, reached the funeral industry in Romania as well. His body was taken through an autopsy to reveal the exact cause of death, then prepared for the burial process by the funeral facility. While the departed was moved to my sister's house by the funeral home with the mortuary limousine, it was still placed in the best room of the house for a two-day viewing. The difference with the casket he laid in, was that it had a refrigerated lid for keeping the constant low temperature. The lamentations and wails, sadness and sorrows expressed by family and friends were the same, as experienced with the other losses we had in our family. Having been a very popular person, Alin's funeral was very well attended, and now he is resting in peace in the family cemetery plot, next to my parents. His loss affected me greatly, as we kept in touch throughout the years after leaving the country, and at one time he had the opportunity to visit us here and spend a couple of months together. He was "my connection" with the country of birth and I spent a great deal of time with him whenever I went back home to visit. A good hearted guy, he finished the Law school in Romania, chose not to take the Bar exam and instead got involved with the business world. While the rest of the family never understood the kind of work he did, he managed to be a great provider for his two children, Fredy and Issabelle. A great loss for us all, but always in our memories.

Living in America since 1982, we had to submerge to the new life here and stay focused on our careers and our family that started expanding with the births of our grandchildren. Without justifying my inability to attend my parents' funerals, on a trip back home after my dad's passing, my nephew Alin (still alive then) and I went to the cemetery to put a wreath on his grave. It was late at night when we arrived there and my brother, not living too far from the cemetery, I sent Alin to bring him there and be with me when laying the wreath on my dad's grave. Shortly after he left, with the flashlight in my hand, I walked in the cemetery toward my dad's grave. In a matter of a minute or so, my flashlight stopped working and I was engulfed by the pitch dark night. To say I was scared, afraid, and on the verge of screaming, would not explain the feelings felt, while waiting in the darkness of the night for my nephew to return in about a half an hour. It was an experience I will never forget, and when returning back home, I took the flashlight to the DOC armorer to check it out as it was my night shooting light issued by the department. The armorer has never found anything defective with the flashlight itself, but we could not make it work again. I believe it was some divine intervention stepping in, to provide me with this unique experience. True or false, I would never know!

MORE ABOUT EDUCATION

It became easier and easier to do well in school as I was finishing middle school in the eighth grade. Learning about so many things and reading a lot, my little world just kept expanding. I had no idea where and what I would be doing in life, but I kept dreaming and imagined that somehow I will find my way in this world. Back then, no further school was required beyond the eighth grade, however, two additional avenues were available for continuing education, with no enrollment cost involved.

The one chosen by most was the vocational programs, that would give the students the opportunity to start working and earning a living by the time they turned nineteen years of age. These vocational programs would have two years of class learning and one of shop time, working as an apprentice in the chosen trade. Compared with what we have in the USA, it would be the equivalent of an AAS program, offered through most of the community colleges. Learning a trade was woven in the Romanian folk wisdom with a strong belief that during one's life many things could be lost but a learned trade could never be taken away. Having learned a trade was also referred to as possessing a "golden bracelet". The only drawback to this avenue was the school's availability only in big cities, like Resita and Timișoara, the residence of our county and the county next door. Attending these programs away from home would involve school boarding expenses and additional sustenance costs. There were some exceptions when the school would support the additional costs, by offering indigent students to live in the school dormitories and have their meals in the school's cafeteria.

The other avenue chosen by the few was enrolling in high school, a four year program of general studies, the precursor to a higher college education. This program would be available in smaller cities as well but not in smaller villages and/or settlements. Most students enrolling in this program would come from well to do families and children of professional parents that understood the merit of waiting eight years before entering the employment arena, with a higher paid professional job (most colleges had four year programs). In a developing country like Romania, this avenue was not considered pragmatic by most people. However, each of the two avenues would require an admission exam with a minimum passing score, as available classes were limited.

Vocational school

Making up my mind about which direction to go for further schooling was just the first step in the new chapter of my life. I say this, because from here on, life started unfolding in many unanticipated ways. Learning early on that accepting things as they happen, rolling with the punches so to speak, builds the necessary resilience we all need when we go through trying times. So, not even sixteen years old, all my friends went to Timisoara Electromotor vocational school and took the admittance exam. The competition was heavy and available seats were limited for one class for each profession taught at that school. From our group, it was only me that passed the exam and was admitted to the class of 1967 industrial mechanics slated to start on September 15.

The anxiety level was high as I did not know much about living in a boarding home, on a limited budget, and fending for myself while attending school. It took a while to learn the bus and tram systems, how to communicate and get along with others in the same predicament, and not having my family close. I was a shy guy, under a heavy learning curve at school and socially. Growing up in the Turcins' family did not involve extensive social etiquette or any considerable level of sophistication. In other words, we lived at "the outhouse/latrine" level. Most of the time I felt inadequate, but determined to learn.

The vocational program was designed for the first year to learn the basics of industrial mechanics theory, learning how to use the tools, how to organize the workplace, safety, and planning specific projects. It was all class time the first year, so at the end of the school day I would go to the boarding home to cook my meals when I did not eat out, and study for the next day. At this time reading was my favorite activity along with going to the movies. The city of Timisoara had quite a few movie theatres and great parks. In spite of all of this, for me it was a difficult adjustment to the new lifestyle. Little I knew then that in life we would face new adjustments constantly. Timişoara was only 160 kilometers (80ml) away from my hometown. My parents would come to see me quite often to bring supplies and I would go home on winter, spring and summer breaks.

While in school, my brother Ion, who was four years older, had finished his vocational school and worked for the copper mine in our hometown as a locomotive conductor. He would take cars full of rock minerals from the mine and drive them out to the plant for further processing. It was during my second year in school when he had a terrible accident and almost lost his right foot. The locomotive derailed and his right ankle got crushed, basically destroying the joint. He was taken to an orthopedic hospital in Timisoara, where he went through a year of reconstructive surgeries. This was very hard for my parents and the entire family. For my brother, being in and out of intensive care for over a year while closing on his twentieth birthday, was not easy at all. Just days from his accident he got the drafting notice for starting his military term and while all his friends went into the military service, he went to the hospital. This frightened, discouraged and depressed him a great deal, and later on we learned that this followed him throughout his life. He had no coping mechanism for such a personal tragedy and was very fragile in his acceptance of the new situation. For my parents it was very difficult to see their oldest child fighting to survive the amputation of his foot, finding the money to pay the surgeon every time there was an intervention, and pay for the numerous trips to Timisoara. Being in the same city, I went to see my brother in the hospital almost daily and started developing a good relationship with him. Prior to this I always felt that there was a big gap between the two of us as he was four years older and we did not have a lot in common. While in the hospital, he fell in love with a nurse's aide named Florica. She was an older woman, divorced and ready to accept my brother the way he was. My parents never accepted her and that was the beginning of a lifelong discord between them. Somehow, years down the road, he forgot what support his parents and myself provided for him through these trying times, and never showed any gratitude, on the contrary, he turned against the whole family. This will be discussed in more detail later on in the story.

In the second year of my vocational school, I was approved to live in the dormitory of the school as I was considered indigent. This was much easier for my parents and also on myself. I shared a bedroom with three other students and learned more about life as I lived it. Having the meals at the school cafeteria, playing volleyball, and developing/strengthening relationships with others my age, made me more comfortable in the new lifestyle I had. There were some young students that had a hard time adjusting to living away from home and one jumped to his death from our dormitory building. It was something new for all of us to learn about life, and the event followed us for a long time as there were no counseling services afforded to us. Ironically, I went through a similar situation about twenty years later after emigrating to the USA and starting my employment with WA DOC. Will share this later on in the story.

By the end of the second year of my vocational school, I was more and more comfortable with the new life in the big city, my new friends, and the factory I was assigned to do the practice at. The name of the factory was Elba and it was profiled on battery making (all kinds), and plastic accessories for lamps, cars, and other industrial use. These two branches with their different production processes were located in the same city, but different locations. I was assigned to the one where batteries were made, as an apprentice to a senior industrial maintenance mechanic. A factory like Elba utilized a diverse machinery system for the stages of the battery making process. Starting with the graphite mixing and ending with affixing labels, our mechanics team was responsible for maintaining the functionality of all machinery utilized. Most of these machineries were imported from other countries and required a great deal of training for understanding their functionality. For this reason the practicum was over a year long. The area where the graphite was mixed in mechanical driven mixers, was the most difficult to work in as at the end of the eight-hour shift our bodies were as black as the graphite in the mixers. The ventilation system was not that effective and the factory supplemented this with a shower for a good scrubbing to clean up. Conveyor belt system, pneumatic equipment, lathes, mills, pneumatic and mechanical presses, they all were part of our maintenance responsibilities.

I do remember a tragic incident when one of the battery cylinder press workers caught on fire as his overalls were imbibed with a gasoline derivate. These gasoline-based products were used to lower the friction effect when pressing the cylinders, that at a later stage were filled with the graphite mixture. The man started running in the factory yard and no one could stop him. He succumbed to his death from severe burns, shortly after. We talked about this accident for a long time and there were many new safety rules and regulations implemented immediately, mainly because many other workers witnessed the incident.

As the time went by, at the end of the third year of school, I very much got used to living away from home, learning how to get along with other people at the workplace, and forging new relationships. My new close friend at that time was Aurel, a student attending the same vocational school and doing his practicum at the other branch of Elba factory. He was from Gataia, a large community nearby Timisoara, about thirty ml west. Living that close to our future workplace, it was easy to accept the invitation to stay with him and his family after graduating. And so I did, and a new chapter in my life has just started.

WORK AND MORE SCHOOL

Graduated from my vocational school in June, 1970 after what seemed to have been a challenge, considering my adjustment to living away from home when I was sixteen and all that came with it. My GPA was not that high, however, I was glad the school was over and I was slated to start work as a mechanic at Elba, the battery factory in Timisoara, while awaiting to be drafted into the military service.

It seems that adjusting to new things became the thing to do from here on. At my new home, I shared a room with Aurel and had no problem with that. In the home there was his teenage sister, his married brother with his wife, and his dad who must have been around sixty years old at the time. As any teenager or I should say a young adult, had many talks with my friend's dad, who liked to drink a little. I don't recall how he lost his wife, but there was a woman by the name of Salomea that would come to the house every day and do the housework. She must have been of close age with him and to this day I remember her talking a lot, with sense or without sense. Later on in life I used her as an example when someone would talk a lot: You talk like Solomea. Aurel's brother worked for the railroad and would go on shifts of twenty-four hours at the time. His wife always made sure he had the food packed and she would walk with him for a while on his way to work. I admired that. Aurel's sister was nice and to this day, I believe he wanted her to get closer to me. She did, however, I never really connected with her and this led to nowhere.

It just happened that in the fall of 1970, when the new school year started, a new continuing education program started to be available in the evening for those wanting to complete their high school. Along with about ten other adults, I enrolled and this was the beginning of another five years of school, excluding the military time of sixteen months. The group of students varied in age and were from all walks of life: the mayor of the city, the police servant, a guy that worked for the railroad, a practical nurse, and the rest were young people that just finished vocational school and wanted to further their education. Some have not been in school for many years so the teachers had to go way back with the curriculum for the subjects addressed to make sense. I forged great relationships with all as we helped each other to find a way to keep up with the learning and pass the required tests.

The days were long and busy. At 6:00 A.M. I had to be at the train station to go to work, a commute of about an hour long. After work, from the train station I went straight to school for another few hours. Somehow we found time to socialize after school, have fun, and get involved in some folk dancing activity. This was totally new to me as in our family, dancing was not sanctioned by the church. I felt good about it, especially when I had my math teacher, also my dancing partner. Others envied me for this. Aside from mutual liking, we did not go further since she was married and had a child.

I started to feel more comfortable away from home, learned how to use the social etiquette, and most of all be comfortable in my skin. I learned rather quickly that different groups I interacted with or belonged to, require different approaches for good functionality.

At work, I had my team of three: me, my partner, and the team leader who was a senior mechanic. Together we would take whatever jobs came our way and had a lot of fun working together. There was a lot of teasing and joking going on with the women working along at the conveyor belts and other stations.

At school, our group bonded greatly while helping each other and going to the tavern after school and during the weekends. My two favorites from this group were the math teacher and the police servant. After I left Gataia for the military service, I never made contact with the math teacher, however, my roads intertwined with the police servant who was promoted after finishing school, to a post at the Border checkpoint by my hometown. While visiting Yugoslavia with my dad later on, he always seemed to have run into Sholea, with whom we had great laughs while he processed our paperwork. My dad always liked that, and I am fond of this memory.

While commuting, we had our group that would reserve the seats and "huddle" while traveling. We joked, we laughed, we teased, and made new friends. Life was good, I went home now and then to visit and help out with things as I could, but I could tell, explicitly, that I did not fit in there as I did growing up. Toward the end of the commute from Gataia to Timisoara that lasted until I was drafted into the military, February 1972, I met a girl that later became one of my first girlfriends. She was enrolled in the nursing school at Arad, a city close to Timisoara, but her parents lived in Resita. We connected right away.

MILITARY SERVICE

On February 2, 1972, 8:00 A.M., after spending the night at my girlfriend's home, I reported for military duty at the recruiting station in Resita, along with a great number of recruits who were as disoriented as I was. The check in consisted of a quick medical check up, getting a buzz haircut, a shower, and a change of military uniform/effects. Not even this date, I don't understand how we got referred to different branches of the required military service, however, I was referred to do my service with the Border patrol. The Brigade was located in Timisoara, with the boot camp located in Arad. Thanks to the life changes experienced prior to this, the impact to the military life was softened. I adjusted quickly to the new lifestyle and I have to say that I liked it. I functioned very well and completed the boot camp with enthusiasm and exceeding marks. I was selected to go to the Drill Sergeant school as a result of my performance, and I liked it. The Drill Sergeant training was demanding, but I was in top physical shape and finished on the top of my group. Somehow the military lifestyle gave me a lot of confidence and if I had my high school completed, I would have continued this career and become an officer. Ironically, it turned out to be a blessing for not remaining in the military service after my required draft, as in 1989, the communist Romania went through a revolution that shattered many branches of the government, including the military. With the drive I had, I would assume that years in the military would have put me at a very high rank, therefore in a vulnerable position.

While in the service, I trained two classes of new recruits and a class of new Drill Sergeants. It was something I enjoyed doing, not only because I thought about structure and tested physical limits, but also reached out and connected with the person. This skill proved to be very useful later on in life, making it easier when I started the Corrections career after immigrating to the USA. Some of my recruits were from my hometown area that later on in life I ended up working with and/or becoming friends with.

In between boot camp sessions, I was transferred to do border patrol at different border stations on the Yugoslavian border. This would have been the work on this military branch if I did not become a Drill Sergeant.

Life on the border patrol was different and required a different state of mind. Depending on the terrain, there were three types of assignments: observer watch, patrol watch and fixed post watch. The observer duty consisted of climbing a tower watch and observing the area to your left and right towers. The patrol watch consisted of a segment of terrain given to you to keep under observation while you move from left to right point. The fixed post watch was just as it says, a fixed position you assumed for a specific area. The soldiers were equipped with an AK 47 Kalashnikov, 7.62x39mm and three magazines of thirty rounds. Before going to their posts, they had to sign in the register the time and the area of the assignment. The interesting fact is that while on duty, they had to face the country and look for the potential "infractors", people that were intending to cross the border to the next door country. As a reward for stopping the infractors, the soldiers were given a leave. I was at one of these locations when one of the infractors was shot while trying to cross the border and the soldier was given permission to go home for ten days. Occasionally, we had infractors that made it to Yugoslavia and were caught there. When that happened, the investigation determined when and at what point the border was crossed by the infractor. Records were kept forever, and going back to the register the soldiers signed in, it was easy to determine who was on duty at the time. Court martial followed, with a jurisdiction of ten years after military service was completed. I did attend one of these trials and the civilian ex-soldier had to go to jail, as he was found guilty of negligence.

While in the service, my parents came to visit me many times, bring some food from home and occasionally some bottles with "plum brandy". While I appreciated my mom's "colac" (walnut pastry) I always turned down my dad's bottles of booze. I suppose I was too dedicated to the cause and that created some confusion and at the same time, admiration from my dad. My dad was a Drill Sergeant also, and he fought in the Second World War. He did understand the soldier's life, therefore my position.

While in the service, I had opportunities to go on leave for the day and one time leave to go home for a few days. One of the things I do remember is going to visit with my g-friend who lived in the dormitory of the nursing school. She seemed to have just left with another guy, as I was told by the staff and other girls at the school. Little I knew that among other girls, there was my Neli who I would marry a couple of years down the road.

BACK TO THE CIVILIAN LIFE

In November of 1973, I was discharged from the military draft to civilian life. I felt strange to the civilian outfit after so long of wearing military garb. After a little while, things got back to a different routine, as deep inside I was not the same person. I felt stronger, with more knowledge about myself and others, and more confident in life. With a good friend of mine, Cozma, who finished his military service at about the same time, I decided to go on a vacation around the country before we got back to work. We visited a few attractions, going by train to different cities around the country and visited with some friends from the vocational schools and the military service. Reconnecting with some of the friends made during the three years of vocational school was an interesting experience. Some ended up working in the field of the chosen trade, and some took a different path in life to help with sustenance for their families. The military service comrades we visited were mainly from our region and it did not take long to reconnect.

The month-long trip around the country was good for both my friend and I. It must have been arranged by divine power, for me to spend quality time with my friend. Within a couple of years, after a vacation to the Black Sea, my friend has not returned home after leaving the Black Sea resort. He was found wandering somewhere in the North part of the country in a disoriented state. While there was no reason to determine what precipitated the quick onset of this condition, he was hospitalized for psychiatric treatment for about a year. His condition worsened, he became delusional and was admitted to the Psychiatric Hospital in Gataia. Immediately after, I visited him at the chronic ward when I was told that his rational mind was gone. It was quite an eye opener for me to see mentally ill patients, an experience I have never had before. After I came to the USA, ten years later, I went back home for the first time and visited my friend at the hospital. His condition worsened, he was in a bare room with just a mattress and the staff would clean him up with a water hose. I still have this sight in my mental memory and doubt that I will ever forget it. A few years later, I found out that he passed away at the age of forty-three.

Life moves on with more changes...

At home, we had a few changes since I left for military service. My sister got married and so did my brother. My sister, Marioara ended up marrying Ionica, a guy she liked and was two years her senior. She moved out of our parents' home to his place where he lived with his parents, about four miles from our place. My brother continued to have a rough time after his mine accident and did not seem to fit anywhere. Through the church, my parents worked an arranged marriage for him with a girl named Lidia, who was three years his senior. He has never loved her, had a rocky marriage, but somehow they are still together.

At the time, a Baptist wedding went somewhat like this: The families got together after they heard of the groom and bride's intentions to get married. This was the case even when the marriage was mended. Customarily, the parents of the groom were supposed to pay for the ceremony, and there were a lot of other pertinent things to agree upon with both parties. For the most part it was a give and take, to keep the young couple happy. The family would hire the most skillful planner and cook and go with that. Usually, the process would proceed with the religious wedding. At this event, a restricted group of family members would go to the mayor's office, who would ordain a civil ceremony and pronounce the couple man and wife. After this, the religious ceremony took place at the church. It was a special service with many prayers, choir singing, poems recited, and the entire service dedicated to the new couple. This was afforded only when both

47

the bride and the groom were baptized, therefore dedicated their life to God in the Baptist religion, or any other. Then the celebration would start. The wedding party would usually take place at the groom's house, where a three course meal was served to the guests. There were some appetizers followed by chicken noodle soup, cabbage rolls, fried pork and chicken with mash potatoes and salad, pastries and many kinds of cookies, and the proverbial wedding cake. The newly wed couple would live with the groom's parents when the groom was the older male child, to further take over the household when the parents got old and incapacitated. As always, there were exceptions to the traditional living arrangements, as when the mother-in-law would not get along with the new bride.

New Line of Work at the Copper Mine

Started working at the copper mine as an industrial mechanic, fixing pneumatic equipment like drilling machines, jack hammers and alike, tools used by miners in their work above and underground. As we had built a shop underground to be in close proximity to the miners, 200 meters under, the work status was "subteran" meaning heavy labor in hazardous conditions, with extra pay and benefits including an early retirement at fifty-five. The team I worked with was great: about five mechanics with a Senior one leading the team. We would man the three shops we had at the mine, with me working mostly at the 200 meter down shop. At the beginning I had my trepidations about working underground. The mine had four levels of galleries in fifty-meter increments. The shaft elevator would take mine personnel in and out and so would do with the cars filled up with the mineral rock. The number of personnel rides were limited as they would interfere with the flow of production. When personnel wanted to go down or up, outside of the elevator's schedule, we simply had to take the ladders. I took them many times and it turned out to be a blessing for my continued physical condition later on in life. We started with carbide lamps that had an open flame, used to get to the shop and back to the surface. At the shop we had electricity and "rezistente", a makeshift heater that kept us warm and comfortable. The work was sporadic and the shop was used a lot as a get together with others working under, reading, and playing cards. At the shop above ground, quite often, we would fry fish on the big potbelly stove in the middle of the shop and drink wine and plum brandy.

Life at the mine was harsh for the miners especially. They worked at the forefront of each gallery, drilling holes for the dynamite blasting, and loading up the ore in the cars that were transported to the shaft elevator by diesel locomotives. The fresh air was brought in by foot and a half in diameter metal tubes, however, the ventilation was not adequate for breathing. The miners had it worse as they were at the forefront of blasting and loading, processes generating additional dust. As a result, respiratory related pulmonary diseases were prevalent. Along with this, accidents happened quite often, most of them fatal, due to poor lighting and lack of safe work conditions. The miners get paid on how much mineral ore they produce, oftentimes trading safety for production, a trade not always in their favor. To "add insult to the injury", the family life suffered a great deal because of the miners' exhaustive work. Infidelities and divorce were prevalent realities, added to the miners' hardship list.

All personnel working at the mine benefited from a shuttle ride to their shifts, including the adjacent town locations. At the beginning of each shift, for those that worked underground "with subteran status" the shift started with a free meal. I don't think this offer was turned down by many. The theft at the mine continued to be a problem, therefore a security system was brought in and gates were installed at every entry way. People got creative and found ways to steal electrical equipment, cement, lumber, diesel fluid, etc. It was not something at a large scale, with people often justifying it "for personal needs". Nevertheless, some were prosecuted, but it was not enough deterrent for others to stop this behavior. This problem I heard continued to the closing of the mining operation in 1990, after the revolution.

Economically, the region started to see quite a few developments: apartment buildings, road improvements, grocery stores, and other services. The entire area was booming and people from other parts of the country kept moving to Moldova-Noua, for work and to get closer to the gate to the West. This was enhanced by the small traffic to Yugoslavia, another avenue to boost the local market with selling things from the west: bubble gum, watches, blue jeans, etc.

MORE SCHOOL AND MARRIAGE

The same evening school that I started prior to the military service in Gataia, was available in my hometown Moldova Noua. Not wasting time, I resumed my classes in September 1974. I was not alone as my good friends Gheorghe and Stefan were with me. Both completed their military service and were ready to make the best of their lives. On the starting day of school in the evening, the boys got seats toward the back of the classroom, a strategy well known to those that did not want to have much to do with the teachers. The irony was that we were in the wrong classroom and we had to move. The girls that were in the front, went to the appropriate classroom and got the back seats. At that point in time I experienced my first conflict with my future wife, who was among the girls taking our seats. One thing led to another and we started to spend a lot of time together. She was a smoker and I, just a social one. We started going out to the movies, walks, and our restricted group parties. It was great and I felt life I have never known before. Right then and there, I knew that she was the one. Took her home and introduced her to my parents, went to her apartment and met her parents, and the relationship got stronger with every day.

By early 1975 we knew that we wanted to be together for the rest of our lives, so we planned to marry. There were some things that I have never thought would make a big difference: religion and culture. My Neli's parents were of Hungarian heritage, working at the same copper mine, and speaking Romanian language with an accent. Just like most Hungarians they were Catholics, while my parents were Baptists. It was impossible to decide what was the appropriate religious ceremony to choose for the wedding. Another thing had to do with what family should have the lead in the process, mine or Neli's?

There was no doubt in my mind that Neli would not be mine, but I still had to navigate through a lot of other things that would have a significant impact on this decision. The family orientation to their religion was at the top. Her family was catholic and granted they were not exactly the "church goers" they labeled themselves Catholics. As you probably know by now, in this religion the newborns are baptized in the parent's creed, so everyone in her family were Catholics. My family was a tad different. My parents were Baptists and were very engaged with their church. In fact, the church provided all social needed interactions for them. I do know this factually, as I was raised basically in that church. There was no other better creed for my parents.

We had relatively good jobs, Neli as an LPN working at the emergency room for the copper mine, and myself as an industrial mechanic for the same mine in the same area she worked at. We both continued attending the evening classes to complete our HS requirements. So, there were a few parallel things going on, and they were manageable.

While courting my future wife, I made friends with the doctor in charge at the Emergency room where she worked. Since we often had fun at the mechanics shop where I worked, meaning we drank wine and brandy while eating fried fish on the pot belly stove, I invited him to join us one time. He did agree, joined us, and it turned out this was not a good idea. The consequences of drinking in excess, is getting drunk. And drunk the doctor was. On top of that, his white doctor's coat was no longer white, as quite a few of the mechanics' shop colors were blended in. Somehow, we managed to get him to his office, where my wife was waiting with a room full of patients. Short of wanting to kill him, the angry waiting patients turned into a mob. It took some interventions on the mine's side to calm them down and reschedule the appointments. It was the last time we invited him to our shop.

On July 28, 1975 we were married by the power invested in the Mayor of Moldova Noua, and pronounced man and wife. There was no follow up with a religious ceremony at the church. Afterwards, we had a family and friends get together at my in-laws' apartment, celebrating the event with good food, plenty of drinks and a great time. I know in my heart that my parents wished for something different, but this was the best I could deliver.

As for anyone else on earth, life moved on with work related happenings or family dramas. Before getting married I knew that there will be some trying times coming my way because of the strong family differences, however, I could have never imagined what was in store for me. I lived it, so I will share it with you as well.

Becoming Parents and Moving On

Our family routine was very much set in this way: We would go to work during the day, spend some time with friends in the evening and during the weekend we would go to my in-laws' for dinner and family social interactions. Once in a great while we would go to my parents' home for the same, because their church schedule would not coincide with ours.

I loved my parents and I was grateful for all the sacrifices they made to raise me safe and sound, but felt terrible for not being able to have them fully part of my new adult life. My work was very flexible with little or no supervision, so during the week on a few occasions, I would walk across the hills that separated the mine from my parents' home and go and visit mostly with my mom who was always home. Those times I will never forget and I am sure my mom did the same. I would have a dish of whatever she was cooking that day and just assured her that things are going well with the new life I have.

Pregnancy is the result of lovemaking and I loved my new wife. Soon she got pregnant, and we were expecting our first child. It was an experience that I will never forget. It was the hope that things will get better with our families and the newborn will bring us peace. Up to this point we were moving back and forth with the family interactions, hardly had any interactions with my sister or my brother, and just minded our lives while working and attending the evening HS classes.

The prep work for the new baby was exciting for everybody. That time we could not anticipate if the newborn was a boy or a girl, we just had to wait and see the divine gift for us. So, on April 12, 1976, we went to the local hospital for our new child's delivery. Things those days in Romania were not streamlined for a smooth delivery. At the same time with Nelly there were two of her girlfriends awaiting the same fate. One of them delivered a still baby on the 12th and that brought the rest of us to an edge. The other delivered her baby in the morning and my Neli had ours after 9:00 P.M. Not being able to be there, it was a great assurance that the new baby girl is safe. After a day in the hospital, we took her home and named her Cristina. We were new parents to Cristina, a healthy baby girl, who was born on April 13, 1976.

What followed should be easily understood: Both families wanted to be involved in taking care of the newborn and we had to decide on what should be done. Not an easy task considering that our families' communication was not that great. Somehow we managed to keep things going, but these "interventions" started to take their toll on our relationship. After Cristina was born, things got worse instead of better. I felt like I was losing the little control I had on my life and my family life.

Historically, this happens to most men now and then, and there are two traditional remedies: friends and/or drinking. I was no exception to this and as a result, started spending more and more time with my friends, especially at the local tavern. It did not help in the long run, but for the time being, it soothed the pain I experienced and helped me forget, at least until I sobered up.

In June 1977 we graduated from HS, evening program, a long awaited accomplishment. This landmark would afford the opportunity to go on and pursue higher education as a long term goal or just move up a notch with the careers we already had. As an immediate result, my wife got moved to the equivalent of an RN position and I was moved to a "technician" position. She continued to work at the same emergency room position she had at the mine, while I got transferred to the contracts section of the same mine. While her work stayed the same with an increased pay, mine was totally different. I continued to keep the same pay I had when working underground as a mechanic, however, the nature of work was much lighter and with even more flexibility.

MOVING UP AND IN THE SAME DIRECTION

Most people agree that life is a continuous adjustment to what happens to us. We were no exception to this rule. We had somewhat more money, more flexibility and more connections with the outside world, while our family interactions stayed the same or got worse as they expected a resolution to the existing conflict.

Since we lived within close proximity to the Yugoslavian border, we were allowed travel privileges to Yugoslavia, the country next door. It was intended for small traffic, within fifty kilometers of the border. It sounds like a small feat, however, this privilege was the envy of the rest of the country. People with these permits had an opportunity to take small merchandise across the border and sell it to the Serbs. With the money earned from the trade, they would buy things that were unavailable in Romania. At the time, things in high demand for the Serbs were: animal salt, croschees, petrol lamps, etc. In turn we would buy Persian rugs, Pepsi, sweets, blue jeans, etc. Fair trade? Only one involved can have the answer to that.

We started taking advantage of this great opportunity and went to Yugoslavia as passengers, with my brother-in-law Ionica and my uncle Gheorghe. They both had cars, but we did not yet. The geography of the neighboring country was very similar to ours, however, for the first time we were taking a look at how life in the west was. People were driving all makes of cars, the streets were lit up with all kinds of flashy advertising, the stores were stocked with produce and goodies presented in the "western way", very appealing to the eye. The streets were illuminated and well marked for traffic purposes day and night and crossing the border, especially at night seemed like we were in a different world. This new world had color while ours was black and white. So, subconsciously life was giving us the subliminal message of wanting to have a better life elsewhere. And we received it well.

OUR FIRST CAR

Riding with friends and taking the bus was our mode of transportation, for going to work or out of town. Not very conducive to comfort or convenience. As said earlier, we were making good money, by the Romanian value of money in the '70s. So we took advantage of borrowing the money needed to pay off the new car we were looking to buy. At the time there was only one make of a new car manufactured in Romania: Dacia 1100 and 1300, a small sedan patented from the French Renault 12. The factory required the cost of the car to be paid in advance and the usual delivery waiting was about a year. With no other choice, we agreed and took the loan for the car cost in order to put ourselves on the waiting list. It was a good feeling considering that in the '70s only about 2 to 4 percent of the Romanian population owned a car. And we did, in the following year.

The car was delivered (to the place to be picked up) in early 1977. By then I went to the driving school (I was twenty-four years old), had a license to drive and I went to pick up our new car, Dacia 1300, mustard yellow in color. It felt beautiful, the way it smelled, drove, and looked. Everyone in our family was impressed as we had a new car in our immediate family. The freedom of our family expanded and we gained a lot more independence. Being an industrial mechanic I had the basic knowledge on how mechanical things work, and little by little, I learned how to maintain and do the necessary repairs to the car. This was my introduction to the automotive program I later took on, after immigrating to the USA. Public transportation was no longer a choice we would make, unless necessary. With my new job, I would drive to different locations that were on my contract list and this would make it more convenient for all. I would get the job done and would be able to buy some merchandise from the area that could be utilized in the small traffic with Yugoslavia. What a great opportunity!

GETTING CLOSER TO THE
WINDOW OF NEW LIFE

I never considered myself a bright individual, my IQ is somewhere about 110, but I seem to have the ability to connect the "dots". I looked at my family situation and the problems it brought to us, and I looked at what I learned about the west and supplemented it by listening to the "Voice of America" radio show. It was somewhat an inspiring talk radio show, especially for someone who was struggling with what was in front of him. The dialog with others was not something one would entertain when talking about this show. The "Securitate police" would track down the listeners somehow and make them face the consequences of listening to the "the west". It was not a patriotic act.

Connecting the dots, with traveling to different parts of the country for work related travels, I started hearing the same concerns from different people living there: We are not doing too good and what is available to buy from the stores reflect it. The reality is that (we found out later) the President and his cabinet decided to pay all the foreign debts the country had, and make Romania an independent country.

The intent was good, however, in the process many people had suffered a great deal. It was widely spread throughout the country with the government tightly controlling everything from the farm to kitchen table, and resistance to this brutal decree often meant imprisonment. People's lives failed miserably. The stores had no valuable merchandise, they sold what was on the shelves. So, it was not uncommon to see only canned fish and vegetables, "tacamuri de pui" in other words the gizzard's package that we can see here attached to a chicken, feet, etc.... The price of gas got higher and not always available. Starting in 1979 a new law was enacted, mandating the car owners to alternate weekends for driving. So, driving a car with license plates ending with even numbers would alternate with the ones ending with odd numbers.

The mining industry was well developed throughout the country as Romania was well known for its mineral resources. The work conditions at the mines were harsh, the safety was laxed and consequently, the miners were subject to many accidents, death, and or pulmonary related diseases. One had to be a person with a strong will power and good health to be a miner. As the living standard was affected by the declining economy, it was the miners that started to revolt the changes from bad to worse. In a socialistic society, like Romania, it was unheard of workers to go on strikes. In the end people simply got fed up because there was nothing to lose by protesting. The miners, however, started to refuse to start the shifts as planned, therefore the expected production was affected. People everywhere started to talk about the public's reaction/sentiment toward the government's plan to export the goods to become debt free and let the population suffer. This became more and more evident in every part of the country, and I witnessed it firsthand as my job would take me to different cities for new contracts on the equipment needed by the mine I worked for.

There was a distinct cultural shift. Entertainment, arts and movies were in line with the new propaganda the government had: to promote the image of the president and the socialist philosophy. The trip to the west was just a dream for the general population, but afforded to the members of the government brass. For the general population, only socialist countries would be a choice, if people could afford the cost.

For us the horizon opened a bit differently, since Yugoslavia was considered the gate to the west. The Serbs were enjoying a prosperous economy as a result of not owning any Second War debts to Russia. President Tito led his country through a guerrilla war against the Germans and won their independence. The private enterprise and the right to work anywhere in the world, brought hard currency to the country, and all enjoyed a civilized standard of living.

A prosperous country, Yugoslavia was considered the "gate" to the west. Many people living in other parts of Romania, planned to relocate to the S/W area of the country for the purpose to get closer to the "gate" with the hope of going west. Some succeeded and some did not. Later on in the story I will talk about an individual who made it successfully to the west.

NEW CAR, NEW OPPORTUNITIES

We were all excited about the new car and new travel opportunities. The following summer we planned a vacation to the Black Sea with another couple friends of ours. It was a great vacation, all-inclusive and all we needed to do was to get us there. So we did. ten days on the beautiful Black Sea beach with three meals waiting for us and no worries on our part. We did good that year and the next year we went back to the same place, as we liked it so very much. Cristina was three years old at the time. For the next couple of years we continued with regular travels to Yugoslavia, selling and buying things that were not available in our country. It would be difficult to comprehend for people living in a country like America, that in those days one would have to go to a different country and buy things for enhancing the living standard. What made this situation worse, was that the communist regime decided to pay the national debt and become an economically independent country. As a result, exporting the prime goods and the natural resources were heavy while the people continue to have access to things/merchandise below the exporting standard.

In 1979, while working at the copper mine doing mining equipment contracts with other producers in the country, I took advantage of an organized trip to Moscow and Leningrad. Unfortunately, Neli and Cristina were left home and I went with a group of another four friends from work. We traveled to Bucharest in my car, that we left with one of Neli's relatives, while boarding the plane to Moscow. It was an exciting time for me as it was the first time I flew on an airplane. I was twenty-seven years old. We spent five days in Moscow staying at a very nice hotel built only for tourists visiting Russia. The visiting routes for visiting the city were pre-determined and we were discouraged from interacting with the Russian people or buying or selling on the public market. We took it as a mere suggestion, and ended up selling our stuff from Yugoslavia and buying Russian goods that were not available in our country. Extra money made went to buying champagne and caviar enhancing our meals. Never had these things before, and it felt good. Among the big attractions in Moscow we visited the Bolshoi circus, famous at the time and ever. In the Red Square we waited in line for hours to visit Lenin's mausoleum and actually had a look at his mummified corpse that was elevated during the visiting hours, from the lab below. Took the Trans-Siberian train ride to Leningrad that lasted one night. We chose to party on the train with hot tea and vodka. Leningrad, just like Moscow, was beautiful with the architecture style, bridges, metro stations lined with marble and the famous L'Hermitage museum. Perhaps Leningrad, more than Moscow, was a showcase of how much the Russians benefited from what came to them as a result of liberating other European countries from the Nazis. The marble, art, cobbler streets, museums were reflecting an abundance/prosperity as we have never seen before. On the other hand, while going to the public markets and local taverns, we had the opportunity to see how ordinary people lived: smoking heavily, drinking cheap vodka and with an unkempt appearance. Not much different from what we have seen happening in the big cities of our country.

This was a very impressive trip that gave me a broader perspective of life, with many memories. I still have a winter Russian hat bought in Leningrad, that you proudly wore when you were little. Ten days went by very fast and back to Bucharest we went to get my car. Got there late at night to find the car with a flat tire and the gas tank empty, while Neli's uncle slept his drunkenness off. I had to restrain my friends from giving him a royal beating. Looking back to the group of friends I took this trip with and more or less my age, they are all dead. My cousin Gheorghe died of leukemia when he was forty-four, Moza died in a car accident when he was about fifty, Gigi and Cico died of unknown medical problems in their mid-fifties.

GETTING CLOSER TO THE PLAN OF LEAVING ROMANIA

We continued living at the same apartment and by the living standard we had then, it felt very comfortable. There was one bedroom, a dayroom with a balcony (we were on the third floor), kitchen with the necessary appliances and a full size bathroom. The central hot water heating system radiated plenty of heat when the cold winters came, and the cement blocks structure of the building kept the apartment relatively cool during the warm summer days. We kept the same jobs with Neli working at the Emergency post for the mine, and I kept doing the contracts that involved quite some travels throughout the country. The circle of friends changed by including another guy, Ionica, who worked with me in the same office. He was about six years my senior and he had a car also. There was not much we did not do together, and I really value our relationship. Continued to remain popular with all as I was easy going, well connected and had a car. If it weren't for the poor family ramifications and the obvious decline in the overall standard of living in our country, I would say that life was good for us. Learned how to better handle the family, mainly by avoiding contacts with most, and started observing closer the disastrous effects of the communist regime.

At work we got a new transfer to our team of five. It was a relatively new mechanical engineer, assigned to our contract team. He came to work for the mine, from the northeast part of the country, with the plan of defecting to the west. I did not know at the time, but the local Securitate got wind of that and started harassing him. As I was connected with people at all levels, I learned that and offered to help him out with facilitating a meeting with the commander of the Securitate for our county. So, at the start of a work day the two of us got in my car and to the audience with the General we went. I don't think he will ever forget this gesture as he was given the necessary harassment protection, became my friend also, and our lives continued to intertwine ever since. Ironically, on our way back from the county hall, I picked up a local guy, whom I knew as working as a police informant. Grateful for the ride given, he confessed to the fact that he works with the local Securitate in trying to frame my friend (who was in the car with us but he did not know who he was) for a defecting attempt. From that point on, I knew my friend will be grateful to me for the rest of his life, and more on this to come later on.

Somehow, the idea of defecting the country started to be more and more appealing. With that still mostly at a subconscious level in my mind, I decided to do a few things differently. We moved back home with my parents, saving considerably on the rent cost, and Cristina started her preschool program in 1980. Focused on her a lot, but the relationship with both our families has not improved. On the contrary, it started getting worse with numerous disagreements, fights and brief separations. I really thought I would lose my mind. I really loved my wife, I really loved my child, and at the same time wanted to show respect and loyalty to my parents who made so many sacrifices to raise me safe and sound. I am very sure Neli felt the same about us and her parents.

I always thought that Almighty gave me some special gift, by subconsciously making decisions that would fit perfectly with the next thing life brought along. Here is an example of what I am saying as it relates to what happened. We still had our car and enjoyed the additional transportation comfort. However, at the time Romania started opening the car market to include options of the Russian-made Lada and Polish-made Skoda. The process of buying was just as lengthy with getting on the waiting list and being ready to pay the vehicle in full when delivered. Being on the waiting list for a new Lada, in the summer of 1981 we sold our Dacia to a well off local restaurant manager. The transaction was relatively simple, I gave him the car and got a bag full of cash. No check system in place then. Now we knew that the decision to leave the country would be the only answer to stay together and raise our child. We were not certain of many things but we knew this: did not want to live in Romania any longer and wanted to live our own life together, without ongoing interference. We really did not have a concrete plan on where we will go, what will we end up doing, nor where.

Had to keep a low profile with this and not talk with anyone, family or friends, about our intentions. Many other people's defecting plans failed because they did just that and the Securitate took care of the rest. A foiled plan usually would result in jail and the lack of any opportunity to succeed thereafter. So, not saying anything to anyone, we paid our debts to whatever creditors we had and found a way to spend some time with the ones we cared about before leaving. Made a special trip to Yugoslavia with my parents, made a similar trip with my brother and sister and exchanged the Romanian money we had left in the German marks, harder and more acceptable currency on the market. We had about 500 marks left after all debts were paid off. To my close friends, I gave some personal things, like a keychain holder, etc. Neli went to stay with her parents at the end of August 1981 and I continued to live at my parents' home. Shared our plans with my best friend Ionica and we arranged for him to drive us to Yugoslavia. At work, I arranged a contract trip to Braila (week long) and spent a couple of days with my parents before taking off.

LEAVING ROMANIA

With all pre-arrangements plans in place, in the mid-morning of a beautiful September day in 1981, Neli, Cristina and I driven by our friend Ionica, started a new chapter in our lives.

With relatively few personal things and legal papers for crossing the border to Yugoslavia, no one could suspect that we were in the process of leaving Romania without plans to return anytime soon. Our plan was to turn ourselves into the local authorities of the nearest major city of Virsitz, asking for assistance to emigrate to the western world. In theory, it was a good plan as we knew that Yugoslavia observed human rights just as the rest of the West. What we did not know was that Yugoslavia had a standing agreement with Romania regarding the travel permits given to those Romanians for small traffic within fifty kilometers of Yugoslavia: This group was exempt from getting emigrating assistance. When told by the local police of this, it was like the sky was falling on us, being faced with either choosing to return to Romania ourselves, or be taken back by them. I suppose we could have considered going back, as we never told anyone about leaving the country, nor giving notices at work. This choice was not at all in line with what we wanted to do: leaving Romania to save our marriage and build a new life together to better the future of our daughter. The other choice would have carried some dire consequences from attempting to defect from Romania.

As it happened before, Almighty took over and helped us choose. It was not either of the choices given, but continuing to go toward Italy and cross the border illegally. And here is how this happened.

At the police station, we communicated with an officer who spoke Romanian when we shared our plans and were given the choices. Unbeknown to us, in the waiting area there was a Serb who knew both languages, and seized the opportunity to make a profit. After we respectfully declined being taken back by the police, we told them that we opted to go back ourselves and left the police station. On the street, the Serb followed us and offered to guide us in taking the bus to the Trieste, the city divided with Italy, as the easiest crossing point without much screening. Being desperate and on the end of the limb, we agreed to buy two-way bus tickets for all four (including him), and take the bus the next day in the morning. Checked into a room at a local motel for spending the night, and were in the company of our friend Ionica for a bit longer.

The following day we said our goodbyes to our friend and boarded the bus with the Serb, to Trieste. I will always remember this dear friend, who passed away about fifteen years later.

The plan, according to the Serb, was to just stay on the bus through the checkpoint as the guards generally do not check papers. It is unbelievable to what extent a desperate man goes in trusting another under certain circumstances. Learned this rather quickly the following morning when we got to the checkpoint with Italy.

After a night-long bus ride and approaching the checkpoint we could see a number of buses ahead of ours and the Serbs' border officers swarming the area. Then and there I realized how big of a fool I was in putting my trust and the welfare of my family in the Serb guide. In Romania I did my military service with the Border Patrol and being trained as such, I should have known that no one is allowed to cross the border checkpoint without proper/legal documents. With the feeling that the ground slips from under me, I was just waiting for Almighty's guidance again. And in a few moments it came.

Cristina got sick and told us that she is just about to vomit. Took her outside and behind the bus, motioning at my wife to follow us. After we took care of Cristina and not seeing other busses behind us, I told my wife to follow me as I took Cristina in my arms heading for the tree line on the roadside. We were far behind in the bus line for anyone to see us getting into the woods. Out of the road site and protected by the trees and vegetation we felt under cover, regrouped and started to work on the next thing to do. We were so close to the Italian border, meaning that we were free to go west when we crossed it, that my initial impulse was to start running toward true freedom. Again, it was not that simple. My wife wore a denim jumper with low heel dress shoes, I wore jeans, and Cristina wore a little jogging outfit. Before she got out of the bus, Neli managed to grab a plastic bag with some change clothes we had for Cristina but left behind the handbag with school transcripts and other documents we had with us on the bus. After we paid for the bus tickets, I still had a few hundred dollars left in my wallet. Looking at the geography of the terrain in front of us I could figure out the direction needed to be taken, however, the trail was not well traveled until we saw a border mark. Yugoslavian border with Italy is not always linear and we found that out when we started seeing more marks at points we did not expect. Then we found a well-traveled trail that we took, and I had a premonition that the trail is walked by the Yugoslavian border patrols on their duty. It was not long until a guard appeared in front of us with a rifle pointed low ready toward us. Knowing that we might still have a chance of being let go, with the little Serb language I knew, I started begging and pointed toward the Italian border. Pointing at the star on his cap, the soldier asked us to walk in front of him toward the nearest border post. When we reached the post, we were tired, hungry and scared that something might happen next. We were put at ease by the post commander who ordered soldiers to feed us and let us rest. The bread, mayo and bologna never tasted so good. I am sure that the universal sympathy kicked in when they had in front of them a family with a small child trying to go free.

Unlike the previous contact with the Yugoslavian police in Virsitz where we had a Romanian translator, at the border post there was no one that knew how to speak both languages. Apparently, the decision was made for us to be taken to the local jail in Cezana, a border town and the closest city to the border post with a translator service. The three of us were put in a larger cell and interviewed by a Romanian translator. We spent most of the day in jail, while the authorities decided what our fate should be. Because we still had a few hundred dollars and it was the weekend with no one of higher authority available to finalize the decision, we were allowed to check into a local hotel until the following Monday. While going to the store to buy some food, it did not take long to realize that we were followed at all times. There are no words to explain the anxiety level we experienced and how scared we were waiting for Monday morning. When morning came, there was a car waiting for us in front of the hotel, with two men that told us to get in the back seat. The car was driven on a winding road that appeared to go back toward the border. Without saying a word to us about what will happen next, the men stopped the car at the bottom of a steep hill and we were asked to get out. When we all got out of the car, one of the men apparently in charge, pointed toward the top of the hill where the border was and said "Italia". It did not take us much to understand that we were allowed to cross the border to Italy. I was so overwhelmed by what I just heard, that I don't remember how profusely I thanked them, took Cristina in my arms and started going toward the border. Not clearly marked and still in the woods, we crossed it back and forth a few times and getting into a clearing we saw some empty sacks taken by the wind that had Italian writing on them. Kept going down that direction and started seeing the top of a settlement down below. We were pretty sure that we were approaching Trieste and walked to the first house we saw asking for some water to drink. The man gave us water and pointed down toward the city saying "Trieste".

With all that happened to us in the last four days, it's difficult to explain the feelings we had knowing that we will not probably be taken back to Romania from this point on. At the same time we were so confused with the unexpected, that we had no idea how to really proceed to make it to Rome and turn ourselves in to the Italian authorities. Also, we started realizing how much we were at the mercy of other people in a foreign land. This was a humbling experience that will never be forgotten. We started the journey of going west with a simple plan, not expecting the daunting emigration process that started unfolding at such speed. Learned very fast that we have to keep rolling with the punches and do the best we can to reach Rome and ensure we are safe. After Rome, we left it for Almighty to decide what's next, and He did.

Walking into Trieste we stopped at a store and bought some snacks, Coca Cola, and cold water. It was toward the end of a warm day and these refreshments felt fantastic. Then we found the train station and bought tickets for Rome. It was a long all night train ride with a lot of worries on my mind, and very little sleep. By mid-morning we arrived in Rome at "Stazione Termini" (last train station). Little I knew then, that this train station will become very familiar to me in less than two months.

Rome and the Refugee Camp

Walking away from the train station among many others, we did not look any different aside from being unsure on what might happen next. By now, living with uncertainty about the next event, has softened some of the anxiety level. Everyone had a purpose and ours was to find a police station and turn ourselves in. Not long after we did find a "Carabinieri station" and went in. Struggling to state our purpose there after a bit, the officer understood and started writing an address and drawing a map for us to follow and get to a refugee office. We learned that it was not the police in charge of processing us for the next step, but the United Nations refugee office.

Somehow, after many inquiries, we did find the office and went in. To our surprise, we found out that there were many others in the same predicament, asking for political and/or economical asylum. With the translator at hand, the intake process was relatively simple as we still had with us the Romanian issued permits for visiting Yugoslavia. After we were entered on the database with the refugee status, we were directed to board the train to the nearest refugee camp in Latina. Back to the train station we went with vouchers in hand for the fifty-kilometer train ride to the refugee camp. With about 50.000 lira on us, roughly the equivalent of $50.00, we boarded the train with a bit of a lighter feeling as a vague sense of purpose in our lives started to shape up.

As we entered the "Campo Di Profughi Stranieri", the name of the refugee camp in Latina and the new ID papers for us were drafted, we just began another new segment of our lives. We were given three choices: USA,

Canada, or Australia, as open to refugees to immigrate to. Learning about America through the propaganda the communist regime broadcasted, we were a little intimidated to go to a place where all the evils are. Canada seemed too cold for us latitude wise, and therefore we chose Australia. And the waiting for the placement process started. What seemed like a rollercoaster of events that unfolded upon us in the last six days, we were coming to a relative stop or considerably slow down at least, when we got a room of our own in a three-story building. Because we were a family, we enjoyed this privacy placement, while the singles, representing the majority of refugees there, were living in the communal setting of men and women barracks. Feeling a bit more comfortable, we started interacting with other Romanians in the same predicament, hoping the placement process will be swift. Our purpose changed from just leaving Romania, to emigrating to a new country that we will call "home" someday.

Life in the refugee camp had its own idiosyncrasy, considering the many nationalities living there while waiting for the next step. Mostly singles, but some families also, the camp population could be easily numbered in the high hundreds. Security of the camp was provided by an office of Carabinieri, located on the campgrounds. The food was available to all, either to be picked up or eaten at the cantina, a large hall with the kitchen staffed by Italian workers and the refugees labor hands. Neli worked there for a little while, just after arriving at the camp. The medical assistance was rendered at the dispensary by the Italian staff. There was a bar also, with cold beer, snacks and Pinball machines, for those that could afford. The toiletries were also available to all according to the need. The only thing not available was some sort of a monetary stipend. There was an interesting informal arrangement addressing this. Latina was a medium size town, located by the Tyrrhenian Sea. The refugees looking for work would line up on the sidewalk of front street and wait there every morning and perhaps during the day. The locals would drive by and stop, asking for the necessary trades to get the job done, pick up the day men or women laborers and bring them back to camp with the day's pay.

In a day or two I got in line with others to be picked up for a job. After a few hours, a few of us got to do some pruning work on a eucalyptus tree farm. Did not like this way of making some money, as it was way unpredictable and unfair. After I learned the word "lavoro" meaning "work", I started walking the streets of Latina and stopping at various businesses and

76

asking: lavoro? Was turned down many times but in the afternoon, I was given a chance by an auto-body shop. The manager took me inside and paired me with one of the laborers to do first stage sanding on a fairly new Volvo 245, damaged station wagon. Not saying a word about pay, started working until the end of the work day. When the day ended, the shop foreman came to me saying: "domani"? Understanding that I was asked if I will be back tomorrow, I said: "si". And this kind of work and communication kept going to the end of the week, when I was paid and told that I could work there as long as I was in Latina. This work arrangement made me feel good and I enjoyed it for about a month and a half. Neli found some work at a restaurant with some other women. Cristina was playing all day with children of similar age and rode her bike. I would come to the camp to pick up lunch, feed her and go back to work. Other parents with small children and not working, watched her when Neli and I were at work. During the weekend, we would go to the beach of Tyrrhenian sea, and aside of "where we might end up in this world", life was good with what we got thus far: We were together as a family, had the emigrating process to Australia started, had a room that we called ours, and most of all, we started dreaming that someday we will find a place that we will call home.

One day at lunch time waiting to get our food, I felt a tap on my shoulder and turning around I saw my ex-coworker and friend, with a big grin on his face. Totally surprised to see him in the camp, I soon learned that about a month after I left, he took my place developing a great friendship with Ionica, my friend that took us to Yugoslavia. Not having the same traveling permit, he was faced with a defect in a different way. With Ionica's help, facing the risk of being caught or die swimming across the Danube, he made it to Yugoslavia, Trieste and the refugee camp. A courageous act made by a desperate young man. He started his refugee life, got in line for daily work, and opted for Australia as well. Our friendship continued developing, and when not working, he watched Cristina for us. One of his jobs there was to bury a dead horse. Him and two other engineers picked up for the job, figured out a short cut to digging a full size whole in the ground for the horse. They ended up cutting the horse's legs to make the job easier. Ever since, we had many laughs on this event's account, that we called "buca di cavallo".

The fabric of the refugee camp had many nations' threads. Languages were different, the color of the skin was different, the behaviors were different. A true mosaic of many nations living together as a small, in transit society. The only similarity every individual and family had, was a dream for a better life in a country different than the one left behind. The refugees in the camp represented a brave group of people with a strong will power to face the unknown in the pursuit of a better life, rather than living a life that got them nowhere in the country of birth. And this is to be admired in our humanity!

The emigrating process to Australia did not move fast and we were told to be patient. We were there for about a month and a half when there was a surge of new refugees that arrived at the camp. Some of the families with children were selected to be transferred to Rome and live in different "Pensiones", hotels that had contracts for these services with the United Nations. Saying goodbye to my co-workers at the bodyshop and my new friends in the camp, we headed back to Rome, getting a room at Pensione Saia. Aside from the new location, our refugee status was the same, we started living in a room at Pensione Saia and got our meals across the street at Pensione Claudia. There were other Romanians there, singles and married, awaiting for the emigrating process to another country to be finalized. Living in Rome was nice, but the new life in a big city like Rome was intimidating. There were no work connections readily available and I started getting stressed out over my inability to provide the extras for my wife and my daughter. Feeling lost, I walked the streets of Rome questioning myself on the emigrating decision we made. And Almighty took care of this again.

In a day or two, I met Gino, an older Romanian established in Rome for many years. He worked as a placement agent for Pensione Clara, located in close proximity to Stazione termini. His job was to spend his time at the train station and advertise Pensione Clara as the best place to check in by the arriving tourists. Those that took him up on this offer, had their bags carried by other refugees that Gino hired, and checked in at Pensione Clara. After a short talk with Gino and desperate for work, he offered me the job. So, my first job in Rome was working for Gino and carrying the luggage of those that selected Pension Clara. I did that for a while and my relationship with Gino improved, especially when he saw that I took my job seriously and never complained. Shortly after, he recommended me to a garage owner for a job of parking the building residents' vehicles in the order they planned on leaving the following day. For my wife, he asked the owner of Pensione Clara if she could work as a maid. Of course our new jobs were "under the table", but had consistency and the schedule was perfect for Cristina's care. Neli started in the morning and I started in the evening. She would leave at 8:00 A.M., when I usually got to the hotel, and I would start at 6:00 P.M., after she got to the hotel.

Felt very good to have this stability of work with such a good schedule and being able to save some money. At my work, I started parking the incoming cars keeping in mind the next day's schedule. The garage would close at midnight and open at 5:00 A.M. I had my own room there with a TV and an alarm clock. Basically, I got my sleep there and was able to spend the day with Cristina. Got along well with Sergio, the owner, who often invited us over for dinner. Senor Pepe, my day shift change and co-owner of the garage, had an open mind to accepting other nationalities, being married to an Ethiopian lady. We got along very well, and sometimes after my shift, I stayed longer there to listen to his stories. Neli's work consisted of cleaning the rooms and washing the linen. Sometimes she worked in the kitchen when told by the Seniora.

In the little time left for socializing, we had the opportunity to meet some other refugees in the same predicament. We shared stories, future plans, and the much needed resources that we could tap in while there. For me it was a great opportunity to learn about other people's lives, getting a new perspective on our humanity and the need to find a common ground for achieving our goal.

BEAUTIFUL ROME

It has been about three months since we left Romania and the life experiences we had in this relatively short time matured us quickly. Leaving the country of birth for not wanting to live there anymore, put us on a new path toward finding a new home somewhere else. It was a daunting task, with so many events precipitating, mostly out of our control. And we did the best we could to stay the course.

With the "new stability" we developed in Rome, life was good again. We had a place to live, we had work that brought us some income, we had our sustenance taken care of by the United Nations, and we lived in one of the most beautiful cities in the world, basically for free. So we started enjoying life in Rome. Shortly after, we bought a bus pass and as time allowed, we started visiting the attractions of the ancient city. In theory, we knew of the history of Rome as we learned for so many years in school. Our country's heritage originated with the Roman Legions left behind in the year of 100 A.D. and our language belongs to the Latin family. So, we focused on learning the Italian language, somewhat similar to the Romanian language.

We found the Trevi Fountain, made in the late 1600s with its waterfalls on the Carrera marble slabs, just as seen in the movie *La Dolce Vita*. We returned to this site many times, being inspired by the marvelous architecture, eating "gelato" and tossing coins in the water pool. The legend says that when you toss a coin over your shoulder in the Trevi's water, you are guaranteed to return to Rome. We still hope to be able to do that again.

We visited the Colosseum, the largest amphitheatre in the world. Built for games, animal and gladiator fights, it had the capacity to seat over 70.000 spectators, with the same view to the arena. Of course the sitting of the elite, (Cesar, senators, wealthy politicians) was upfront, where they could have smelled the burning flesh or the blood spilled at fights. The rest of the citizens filled the remaining four levels, but they never had to pay an admission fee. In those times when the Roman Empire commanded the world, the fights and shows were many and impressive. In 1981/82 when we were there, there was no admission price to see the ruins of this architectural marvel, and we went back many times, learning something new every time we returned to the site. The movie *Spartacus* depicts the Colosseum in its historical splendor. One time, I went there with my friend, who was transferred to Rome after we did. With no security involving personal searches, we sneaked in a bottle of Vermouth, drinking it on the slabs of the fifth level that had fewer visitors. We considered that historical also.

The Jewish catacombs was an impressive attraction as it involved walking the galleries about ten feet underground. The quiet, the significance of the holy burial ground, and the sight of some remaining human skulls, was impactful and at the same time eerie. The other mausoleums above the ground were majestic and very well depicting history scenes. The Trajan column, erected to represent the Emperor Trajan's triumphant conquest over the Dacians, was very significant for us as it depicted battle scenes that resulted in the development of what our country became.

St. Peter's Basilica in the center of the Vatican is an architectural wonder that no traveler to Rome should miss. A marble structure and precious paintings with so much history depicted, very easily tops all that one can see in Rome. The Sistine Chapel with Michelangelo's paintings leaves one in awe. The artist's struggles while commissioned by the Pontiff to do this work are very well represented in the movie *The Agony and the Ecstasy*. David's sculpture, Madonna's painting, and many other mythological heroes' sculptures and paintings, seem to be everywhere in the Vatican. The view of Rome from the top of the Sistine Chapel is breathtaking. Seeing this all, made us so humble, thankful to Almighty for giving us a chance to see the history we learned about in school. What a great gift.

In 1982 we went to the Vatican for the Easter celebration. It was Pope John Paul the II's first public appearance after his assassination attempt in

1981. No need to say how many people attended, but the entire plaza in front of the Basilica was filled up. Approaching the blessing lines of the Pope and his Cardinals, Neli got separated from me and Cristina. Through some miracle, keeping Cristina by hand next to me, we ended up in the Pope's blessing line. It was so overwhelming when the Pope reached and touched our foreheads blessing us, as he was doing with all who were in his line. I will never forget this special event and later, after arriving in the USA I got baptized in the Catholic religion. More on this event later. We have a memorable picture of the three of us taken in front of the St. Peter's Basilica at the Vatican. It was very expensive and I remember having to make two payments to get it. Enlarged and framed, it will always be with us in our home, representing a memorable event in the journey of coming to America.

COMING TO AMERICA

While we enjoyed seeing the splendor of Rome, we were still concerned about the emigrating process to Australia being put on hold. Cristina came to be six years of age in 1982 and we were concerned with her missing school if we waited for Australia any longer. Again, faced with deciding between Canada and America, we chose America believing that Almighty will guide us as He did thus far. In about four months, while working and keeping up with visiting Rome's attractions, we had all the medical exams and the American consulate interviews completed. Finally we were accepted by the American consulate with the refugee status, and were given a departure date of middle of August 1982, to Spokane, Washington. Not having any connections with family, relatives, or friends in America, it was the World Relief's decision to place us in Spokane, where the Catholic Charities found a local Pentecostal church as sponsor for us. Looking at the map and seeing that Spokane is somewhat at the same latitude with Romania, we agreed, and understood that at least we are familiar with the four season weather. At that point in time we had never anticipated how difficult the language and cultural barriers would be for us, until we arrived in America.

In about a year's time since we left our country of birth, we had said our goodbyes quite a few times to our new friends, as we moved from place to place. We met wonderful people who helped us along, we made friends with many who were in the same predicament, and we were taken advantage of by others who were looking to profit from our ignorance. We saved most of our earnings and by this time, we made a Million. That is Liras and not Dollars, which would be about $1,000.00. Nevertheless, we felt rich! All in all, our new life started giving us unforgettable experiences and a resilience much needed in the new country we will soon call home.

With other refugees accepted by America, we boarded the plane to New York. In those days of the early '80s, smoking was allowed on the plane, and so was drinking. Remember having quite a few drinks with the people I would not see again, as each one had a different destination. At landing we said our goodbyes again and met our escort that took us to a nearby hotel for the night. I will never forget how big the cars and the hotels/buildings appeared to be. In Italy the majority of cars were of compact size, with Fiat 500 predominantly. The pensiones and buildings in general were with distinctive appearance but relatively small compared with what we found in New York. A somewhat funny moment was the quest to find the toilet flushing button, positioned on top of the water tank and covered with a decorative rug. In most places we have been in Italy and the rest of Europe, the water tank for the toilets was detached and activated by a pull down chain. And so the new learning has begun. Having been given food vouchers, we went to the hotel's restaurant for dinner. It was really at that time when faced with our inability to articulate what we would like to order, when we realized the challenge of the English language. After a restless night, back to the airport we were taken for flying to Spokane. There are no words in describing the anxiety level we experienced while not knowing what to expect of Spokane and the people we were about to meet.

SPOKANE, WA – OUR NEW HOMETOWN

After two segments of flight from New York, we arrived in Spokane in the evening. At the airport we were welcomed by Catholic Charities representatives, a Hungarian translator, and the family from the Pentecostal church that agreed to take us to their home until we would get the refugee assistance started. Tired, overwhelmed with mixed emotions about being at the mercy of others, not able to express ourselves in English, not knowing what the next day might bring us, we were taken to our sponsors' home. After all others left, we were placed in the basement of the house where they had a room with a mattress and bedding for sleeping. Thinking of this arrangement as being very temporary, we braced in for the new segment of our life in America. The sponsor family were nice to us and they had two daughters a bit younger than Cristina. The father had another daughter from his previous marriage, a teenager who chose to live with someone else.

With the help of the Hungarian new friends and some Ethiopian new friends who spoke the Italian language, we started learning about the welfare system and community resources available to those in need. Eager to live by ourselves, in about a week we got our welfare assistance going and moved into an apartment not far from our sponsors, in Spokane. As a family, our welfare assistance was about $400.00 cash, $125.00 in food stamps, and the necessary medical coupons. Compared with what we made in Romania, our income tripled just in about a week after immigrating to America. What a deal, we thought.

After learning how to take care of the rent and other utilities, food cost and clothes, transportation cost, we figured just like our new Ethiopian friends, that Value Village and Goodwill have a lot to offer. Reminded on an ongoing basis that learning English was of paramount importance, Neli started going to Bancroft school for English as a Second Language (ESL) in the morning and I would go in the evening, for Cristina to have care throughout the day.

Going to church was something very important for our sponsors and we were taken along every time. The congregation was nice to us and other ethiopian refugees, but the Pentecostal religion was not a choice of ours. Thinking back at how big of a factor our family religious orientation played in leaving the country, made it even more difficult for us to accept and fully participate.

A family from the church had a welding supply business and agreed to hire me as their repairman, refurbishing the welding torches and apparatus. I accepted and started working on a SITA (State Income for Training Assistance) contract, where the government would pay half of my wages and the employer the other half. A very good deal for the employer who paid me $2.50 per hour.

I was given a ten speed bike from a bike shop owner at the church, and used it as my transportation everywhere. While Neli got a bus pass and used public bus transportation, I biked myself everywhere I needed to go. The bike was an old one, and it was quite often that I made the trip to the bike shop, to have broken spokes replaced. I do remember fondly of how the bike shop owner always smiled at me and assured me that all will be okay, while he replaced the broken spokes at no charge. Somehow I ended up buying a coupon book, advertising free items at various locations throughout Spokane. I remember vividly a trip I made to a food store close to Trent and Sullivan Rd. to get a carton of eggs for free (about ten ml one way). When coming back on Trent, just past the old St. Vincent De Paul thrift store, somehow my front wheel got into the railroad groove and I fell. With me of course the eggs hit the ground, and one can guess the rest. I got a great lesson on what it means to "add insult to injury". Setting things like these aside, the bike came in pretty handy as it helped me get to know Spokane, went back and forth to work, and kept me in shape.

Once again we started to feel the relative sense of stability, with an apartment of our own, some social assistance for at least eighteen months, a job for me that paid $5.00 per hour, Neli and I taking ESL classes, and Cristina going to her ESL school, first grade. Through our Ethiopian friends, we learned about the subsidized apartments being available, got on the waiting list and got approved for one within a month. Breaking the lease and forfeiting the deposit, we moved into the Columbia subsidized apartment on East Hartson. Things started looking up, the rent was half of what we paid before, all utilities were free, and there was daycare available for Cristina. Also, we had our Ethiopian friends living in the same complex, making it easy to visit, socialize, and for Cristina to play with their children at the playground. The Columbia subsidized apartment complex had about seven apartment buildings, rented to different immigrant nationals and locals in need of rental assistance. The fabric of the population there included whites, blacks, Ethiopians, Chinese, Native Americans, etc. On the third floor of our apartment building we had a large family of Native Americans as neighbors. With loud music and frequent fights, the police cruisers were present quite often in the area. One night our front door got knocked open by the weight of a fallen woman rolling down the stairs, and one day we found a young child of six to seven years of age sleeping in the balcony of our apartment (we lived downstairs). With occurrences like these, it did not take long to realize that the area was not the best in town, however, we did not get involved and looked at the positives of that residence.

The job did not last beyond the SITA contract of sixty days, but now we were determined to get the American dream. With that said, we turned our focus to education and learning the English language, aiming to make it good here. Had about $1,000.00 brought from our savings in Italy, made some money here and with what we saved from welfare assistance, we had enough to buy a used car. Knowing how to drive a car was not something new to me, so getting the driver's license was easy. Our first car was a Buick 500, two-door coupe. The air intake came through the hood into the air vents for a Quadrajet carburetor feeding a 350 cu.in. motor. Loved that car and just like the first car in Romania, it gave me more confidence and the freedom to go places with my family.

Continued to live in our subsidized apartment, taking ESL classes, enjoying the relationships with the Hungarian and Ethiopian friends, getting immersed in the American culture, learning the English language, and dreaming big. If we were homesick at the beginning of our journey and questioned the decision of leaving the country of birth, now we were beyond that point. It became clearer to me that we made the best decision to leave the country of birth and as a result, our horizons started to broaden. While fully aware of many other obstacles we will have to overcome, we kept looking at what we accomplished thus far: We learned that every person we have met had something different to offer, we learned how to converse in many languages, and most importantly, we learned how to navigate unfamiliar locations. Our goal list was long, however, school was number one on our agenda with the first step to pass the ESL test and enroll in the community college.

Our friend ended up in Portland, where World Relief found a sponsor for him. We kept in touch, and after he bought his own car, he came to visit us in Spokane. We learned that he connected well with the large Romanian community in Portland, opened up a Wrought Iron fabrication business, and started building wrought iron fencing. I did go to work with him during a school break, and that helped us financially a bit. The second trip to Portland I made, was after he got married to a Romanian girl, about eight years his junior. With a short temper, he got in a fight with his in-laws and threatened to shoot them. His wife called me for help, and in a matter of six hours or so, I was in Portland, diffusing his anger. Took his .20 gauge shotgun, and back home I came.

It turned out that my friend made his marriage work well, they became parents to three wonderful children, started an adult family business, and became financially successful.

MORE SCHOOL AT SCC

In about five months' time, our English language proficiency allowed us to pass the ESL test and enroll at Spokane Community College, taking further math and English below 100 level. The grammar aspect of English was not that difficult for us to comprehend, however, the pronunciation became quite a challenge. Conversing with our newfound friends was much easier, mainly because we faced the similar pronunciation struggles. With others, we kept the dialog short and were somewhat fearful for not understanding, or not being understood. It is interesting how this could affect one's self-esteem and confidence, greatly impacting the social interactions.

Being realistic with our inability to speak English correctly, I aimed to enroll in the Automotive AAS program and Neli in the Nursing program. We hoped to be able to do better in these programs as we previously completed them in Romania. Also, it became apparent to us that learning the trade language and getting the needed certifications will enable us to gain more permanent employment with better wages.

At thirty years of age and respectively twenty-eight, we started enjoying our social life with our newfound friends here. We were happy for Cristina having children of her own age to play with and a Day Care and playground were a welcome addition to our peace of mind. Continued taking different required classes for our intended programs at SCC, throughout the Spring and Summer quarters of 1983 school year. Although grateful for our sponsor family's generosity, because of our drastically different religious orientations, the relationship started waning. We attended less and less church services, but I did respond to going on a trip to Seattle to meet with some Romanian immigrants that joined a similar church there. One of them was Corny and the other Ion. They both defected from Romania in the spring of 1983 and left behind their wives and children, with the hope of reuniting soon. It was a good visit, and talking Romanian with people that came from the same region of the country, felt very good. Later on, we continued our communication, became good friends and started visiting whenever we had the opportunity. Their families came to join them, had more children, and started taking whatever jobs came their way as further school was not part of their goal. Corny became a lifelong friend to us and we still have weekly phone conversations in Romanian language.

Completing all requirements, I was accepted to start the Automotive program in the Fall of 1983 and Neli started the Nursing program in January of 1984. We did consider this a landmark on our journey to success and applied ourselves to do the best we could. Both of us were granted financial aid and had work study as a supplemental income. I was working in the shipping and receiving and later doing janitorial work and cleaning, maintaining automotive equipment when I started the Automotive program. Neli had her work study at the Botanical Greenhouse of SCC. Made some good friends with some classmates and instructors, always curious about my heritage and culture. Standing out with the way I spoke English, some did make fun of me and if in the beginning I took it personal, slowly I started understanding that I had no control over this. My performance in the Automotive program was excellent and I was grateful for having completed the Industrial mechanic three-year training in Romania. Working hard at whatever projects we had, I was very much liked by my instructors, who always quarreled over having me do work study for them. Became family friends with Tom the engine instructor, Earl the electrical instructor, and Bert the transmissions/transaxle instructor. Good people, very supportive, always remembering them fondly. Making it to the last quarter with a 4.0, I was recommended for completing the last quarter of the program On the Job Training (OJT) at Barton Volvo Jeep Dealership, located in Spokane Valley.

I can't express enough gratitude toward this group of people that were genuine in accepting our family in their lives, and offered their friendship and support we so much needed. I remember a man from the church, after finding out about starting the Automotive program, gave me a $100.00 bill to help with buying the needed tools. What a gracious act! I made a promise to myself to do the same, and pay forward as often as I can.

AUTOMOTIVE WORK

In the spring of 1985, I started my last quarter of the automotive program
with the OJT status at Barton Volvo Jeep dealership. I was responsible for
the Lube stall and doing revisions on the used cars that were received from
the trades made. My stall was next to Al's, a seasoned Volvo mechanic who
liked to work in the very back of the shop, where our two stalls were. Al
was an interesting individual, with whom I "clicked" immediately. A
Vietnam vet, long beard and extensive life experiences, Al helped me
tremendously with the diagnosis of the automotive issues. We had extended
dialogs about our worldly experiences and we became good friends. His
wife, Sarah, was a student at Eastern State University (EWU). It is
interesting how later on, after I changed careers we reconnected with Al
and Sarah, learning that Al opened a small shop on his property in western
Washington and Sarah worked at the nearby prison as a treatment provider.
Stopped by their home on a few occasions to visit. What wonderful people!

Proudly, I graduated from the two-year Automotive program, with an
AAS degree. Continued working at Barton dealership, completed additional
technical training for Jeep vehicles and was promoted to a journeyman Jeep
technician. My flat rate pay increased to $12.85 per hour.

When Neli graduated with an LPN degree, she was hired by Valley
Crest, a long term care facility in the Valley. She started with a pay of $6.00
per hour. With both our jobs in the Valley and a steady income we no longer
needed the welfare assistance, and moved into another apartment in the

Valley. While grateful for the state subsidies when we needed help, we were proud to be able to take care of ourselves by being enrolled in the professional workforce. Not being entirely satisfied with my English proficiency, I continued taking evening classes at Spokane Falls Community College. The days were long, took a lot of effort to keep up with both and find time to be a parent, but going early to bed and early to rise, I managed.

FROM IMMIGRANTS TO SPONSORS

We kept in close contact with our families at home, mostly our parents, by phone and frequent writings. One of my first cousins, Gheorghe, also really wanted to emigrate with his family to America. We basically grew up together, were of the same age, had the same names, and our fathers were brothers. It did not take long for the red tape to bring them here, and within about a year we had family relatives living next door to us. Their son, Valentin was a few years younger than Cristina, but they got along well with each other and we were happy to have them with us. They went through the same struggle with learning English and within almost two years he could not find employment in the area. An electronic engineer by trade, familiar with the mine exploitation operations but not speaking the language, he started looking for employment at different locations out of state. Shortly after, he was hired by Newmont Gold, an open pit gold mining operation in Elko, Nevada, as an electrician. Later on, Gheo found employment with Fisher Electronics in Philadelphia. At the age of forty-three he was diagnosed with leukemia, an affliction he succumbed to at the age of forty-four. We visited a few times while he was still in remission and on a family trip to Toronto to visit some of his friends, we stopped to marvel at Niagara Falls. What a nature wonder! My third trip to Philadelphia was to attend his funeral and deliver the Eulogy. It was a sad day to see him gone, and for the second time I have seen the name of Gheorghe Turcin on a cemetery cross (first time was my brother's in

Romania). So, after a short time with extended family, we went back to being just us.

Took advantage of a great opportunity to move into a ranch style house located in Spokane Valley, a house that belonged to a Romanian guy that used to work for Kaiser plant in the Valley. Willy was in the process of moving to LA where his family was, and needed someone trustworthy to manage the property and pay some toward the rent cost. This was a great move up with the living standards: great neighborhood, spacious house with a large finished basement, two wood fireplaces, large yard, and an attached two car garage. Life for us, just got better. I had a great job working as an auto technician during the day and going to additional classes after work, Neli worked nights, and between the two of us we took care of Cristina's needs. The bank account reflected the hard work, and the savings started going up considerably. Not too much of a social life any longer, but we felt that we were making considerable progress overall.

Learning the English language was a daunting task, to say the least. Going on six years now, we just started to absorb the language directly, not having to translate the meaning into Romanian and then back to English. This is something that delayed the response, often making us look silly while conversing with others. So, we dove into it and taking a beating at times, we kept moving forward. I definitely wanted more, therefore kept going to school in the evening.

As we lived our new life in America making a slow but sure progress with our enculturation, and thinking about how impactful it was when I got blessed by the Pope, decided to become a Catholic. Neli welcomed this decision, as she and Cristina were baptized in this religion and I had none at the time. While hoping for my parents' understanding, who always wanted me to embrace the Baptist religion, enrolled in the Catechumen program at Sacred Heart parish as a non baptized person. It was a pleasure to meet Father Joe, who spoke some Italian also, as he spent considerable time in the Vatican training programs. Do not remember the exact length of the program, but I do remember Connie, my guide for this program. She was kind and understanding of my language barriers, patiently teaching me the Sacraments of initiation. Finishing the Catechumen training, I was baptized, confirmed and received my Eucharist. So I joined my family through the path of the Catholic religion. My parents showed understanding and acceptance of my decision, when I wrote them about it.

Becoming Americans

Having met the required five years in the USA, we applied for our citizenship and went through the procedural interviews. It took about six months for the process to be completed, and on January 15, 1988, we took the oath of allegiance and became naturalized U.S. citizens at the federal court in Spokane, Washington. What a grandiose moment! Six years of continuous hard work, trying times, and a lot of focus, paid off. We are now belonging to the best country in the world, the USA. Every effort we put in to reach this landmark, was well worth it. Somehow, I always thought that the first step in reaching the American dream was to become an American. And we conquered it! The rest, as we found out, was entirely up to us.

Choosing to move to the next level closer to the American dream, continued working and taking evening classes. In June 1988 graduated from SFCC with an AA degree. Feeling more confident with the ability to speak English, Neli and I agreed that I should pursue a higher level of education while she will continue working as an LPN. Started exploring some of the majors available at EWU where I could use my earned AA degree, and started the major of a BA program directly. The Criminal Justice program looked very appealing to me, as an old desire of mine was to work in Law Enforcement. Learned more about the available program after I met with Professor Moynahan, one of the two advisors available. I was very much advised and supported to pursue this program, mainly because of my age (thirty-four) and my life experiences. However, the complexity of the three Law classes needed to be taken in the junior year, would require me to dedicate my entire time to school and stop working.

Deciding on following the advice of Professor Moynahan, enrolled in the CJ program at EWU with a start date of September 1988. After applying for financial aid and Stafford school loans, I stopped my employment as an Automotive technician, and took a month-long vacation driving my family to Disneyland.

Somehow, we found our way all the way to San Diego and back. I experienced high anxiety levels while having to navigate through the Interstates, with paper maps that most of the time confused us. Driving through the Death Valley was an experience that I will not forget. Having to adjust the timing on my car when the motor started pinging, got hit by the hot air that must have been over 100F. The car had a functional air condition system and prayed to keep working, and got out of the area as soon as we could, not taking the time to see other attractions in the area. Later, we learned that the Death Valley is 280 feet below sea level, with record temperatures of 134F.

Disneyland attractions were totally worth visiting, and we all felt like children in an enchanted land. After spending a few days there, we drove to the San Diego Sea World. The exotic animals and birds on display, the seals, dolphins, and whale shows, were beyond belief to us. We were so grateful to Almighty for guiding us on the path of learning how to reach the possibility and see these wonders. And just like from all vacations, we got back home and ready for a new school year for Cristina and I and back to work for Neli.

CJ PROGRAM AT EWU

With lots of trepidations, in the fall of 1988 I started the CJ program with a junior status. The classes taken, starting with Technical writing, Basic Law, Criminal procedure, etc. were challenging, to say the least. Developed good relationships with other classmates (Steve and Scott), and started studying together, making understanding of certain concepts easier. The days were long, with a lot of time dedicated to practically memorizing a good part of the curriculum. However, we found time to celebrate our little successes, spend time with the family, and kept hoping for the best.

At the end of the junior year, we had to find an agency of our choice to complete the mandatory Internship (400 hours). Not even today, I can't explain how I set up an appointment to meet with the Superintendent of Pine Lodge Pre-Release facility located in Medical Lake. Superintendent Bob, whom later I found as a consummate professional, discussed my school program, goals I had with the intended profession, and offered me a private tour of the facility. Jokingly, Bob told me that he could not help but see me react in a different way, when opening and closing the cell gates. And he was correct with that! He followed up saying that the field of Probation and Parole would be a much better choice that I should make. He further referred me to a couple of officers he supervised in the field, when he worked there. And that's how I met Denny, a senior officer in the Intensive Management Unit of DOC field office in Spokane. It was just before Christmas of 1988, when I got enrolled as a volunteer to help Denny out however I could, whenever I had some time to spare. It was one of the best decisions I made, career wise. The work in that office eased me into the world of Corrections, learning about the worst of human behavior. Denny and I became good friends, a friendship that lasted into our old age. It wasn't long until the circle of friends expanded, others took a liking to me and asked for help with car repairs, which I gladly did. My English improved, my confidence got stronger, and I felt that slowly I am moving into the next level of the professional world.

In the summer of 1989, with the approval of my adviser at the CJ program, I began my internship at the same DOC field office with Denny. Started making jail visits with arrested offenders, gathering information for the court reports, attended court and board hearings, participated with limited involvement in arrests, searches, and the necessary transports. I was doing very well, and impressed my CJ program adviser with the Internship evaluation I earned, to the point of him asking if I am interested to become his TA (teacher aid) in my senior year. That I promised!

At the end of my internship, and evaluated as making excellent progress, I was offered an emergency hire position, as a Community Corrections Officer 1 (CCO1), covering a caseload that was not managed for a while as the supervising officer was on extended sick leave. That was September of 1989. After seven years in America, under Denny's closed supervision, and working with the rest of the CCOs in the Unit, I started my temporary employment as an officer of DOC.

If I was busy before, my days got longer now, adding my full time employment to the required school work. Continued to do well in school, as a student and a TA to Professor Moynahan, and splitting my work schedule to accommodate the school schedule. I must have applied myself and performed well at work, as the thirty-day emergency hire position was renewed after a daybreak in service. And this happened every month, until I graduated in June of 1990. My friends at work never missed a chance to celebrate my hiring every month, when I had to buy the beer at Charlie my Boys, our well frequented pub that was next door to the Court house. "Stopping for one" proved to be a great benefit to develop additional relationships with prosecutors, defense attorneys and Judges. It was not uncommon for us to strike deals on violation recommendations, with the prosecutors and defense attorneys while having a beer together. Judge Jim, Bob, and bailiff John joined us there quite often, and learning about my temporary employment, Judge Jim and Bob, wrote a letter of recommendation to the Field Administrator of our DOC field office. I am sure the letter of recommendation had a lot to do with the Field Administrator offering me a permanent hire position as a CCO after my graduation. Through the years, as I moved on with my DOC career, I never missed a chance to express my gratitude to these people that believed in me and supported me along. Regrettably some of them are no longer with us, however, never forgotten.

In June of 1990, after eight years in America, I graduated from EWU with a BA degree in Criminal Justice. Also received the highest award for accomplishment in the program: V.A. Leonard award. I credit many people for being able to reach this landmark: my wife Neli, Denny, Chris, Jim, Bob, and many others with whom I continued to remain friends into old age. Denny and his wife hosted the graduating party at their home, where all our DOC and Automotive school friends were invited. With the help from so many people and many personal sacrifices, in the course of eight years in America, we furthered our education, became American citizens, and held professional jobs. What a great accomplishment!

OUR PARENTS' VISIT TO AMERICA

With both of us holding professional jobs, living in a nice home, and with a good income, we decided to bring our parents here for a three-month visit. The process was rather simple then, and after sending the invitation for the visiting visa and the purchase of the plane tickets, my parents came here in the summer of 1991. We have not seen each other for ten years, and there are no words to explain the joy and happiness, greeting them at the airport. For three months, we enjoyed the visit at home, took them on trips to attractions around the Spokane and Seattle area, and gave them the opportunity to see us accomplished in the new country we call home. My parents were very religious and respecting that, I made a point of taking them to a different church for service every Sunday. They did not speak the language, but they could relate peripherally, as church services have similarities. That made them happy, and made me happy as well, to be able to show a token of appreciation toward raising me sound and safe.

My parents realized how big of a challenge the language was, and when we offered to keep them here with us, they turned down the offer. So will my in-laws. They were in their early seventies, and did not want to relocate to a place where they could not communicate with others. It was at the end of summer when I ordered a cord of wood to be delivered to my home and a situation at work kept me there late, Neli was at work, and only my parents were home. To my surprise, when I got home, my dad and the delivery guy staked the wood in the backyard and they were talking, each on his own tongue, waiting for me. Somehow I could see myself in a similar situation after arriving here and not speaking the language.

Two weeks after my parents went back home, Neli's parents came for their three months visit, just in time for Thanksgiving. We did the best we could to take them sightseeing, just as we did with mine. I remember taking my father-in-law with me hunting at Skookum and giving him the opportunity to shoot my 3.08 Winchester. My hunting skills have never brought us a deer, however, on that trip I shot a rabbit that basically was torn apart by the powerful bullet. Later on after they went home, I kept him informed how unsuccessful my deer hunting trips were. His response was that I should go hunting for rabbits instead. Touche!

Somehow the return tickets for them required to fly out of San Francisco. So, I flew with them there and spent a day in the bay area. Had enough time to visit the Alcatraz prison with them before they left. My father-in-law was so impressed that he talked about this until his last days. Bringing our parents to visit was one of the best gifts we could have given them, and to ourselves. It was just a small token of appreciation for our parents that raised us, oftentimes struggling with the demands.

Cultural ramifications

Cristina was developing well and turned into a beautiful sixteen-year-old. We were so happy of her adjusting to life here, and in our desire to learn the English language we did very little to teach her Romanian. Getting enculturated was a bit more difficult for us and accepting certain things sanctioned by society here, brought us a serious conflict with her. She fell for a guy at her HS and started not following our parental guidance any longer. We tried counseling together, to no avail. The counselor suggested to let go and accept, but this was something we could not do. We left our country to build a better life for her, and being clearly on that path we just could not see her not doing well in school and spending a lot of her time with this guy who was not a stranger to the juvenile system. We lived with this kind of conflict for about two years, and it tore us apart. Somehow she had enough fortitude to enroll in the running start at SCC and graduate her HS at East Valley.

When she turned eighteen, we convinced her to get her CNA license and start working at the same workplace with Neli. Almighty answered our prayers again and she started a friendship with Marshall, an LPN at work. Her previous relationship with the juvenile delinquent started waning and very soon she did not want anything to do with him. However, he kept harassing them both, and we came to an agreement that they should move to the Tacoma area, for her to enroll in the nursing school Marshall just completed a couple of years before. We helped them with the move in an apartment close to the Clover Park nursing school near Marshall's parents home in Steilacoom, gave her one of our cars, and continued to support her while going to the nursing school.

Building a home in America

Working with a great group of people and developing a new social network, brought new friends in our lives. It was in 1990 when I met Garry B., a general contractor who will become a lifelong friend. He was living in the same area where we lived, in an apartment complex south bound of us. Recently divorced, he lived with his girlfriend Cathy who was recently divorced as well. They would join our group of friends whenever we stopped for a beer before heading home. Through him I learned that the company he worked for, Northern Enterprise, had lots for sale in the Newman Lake area where he was building houses for customers that had bought lots there. The lots were about similar in size, 1.5-2 acres, and Neli and I decided on buying one. The way we rented the house we lived in was inexpensive, but we wanted to have a house of our own in the new country we called home now. Agreeing to the price of $22,000.00, in 1990 we became the proprietors of the lot located in the Newman Lake area, while still renting the house on Grace. Not being quite ready to build a home, we kept working and saving toward building a home.

We reached that point in 1992, when Garry agreed to the building of our home. By that time, Garry and I became good friends and broke the ground for the foundation of our new home. It was customary in our culture to throw some change in the ground freshly excavated and champagne toast to future prosperity. Gary and Cathy were impressed with this, and started telling other friends of how we look at these things culturally.

I was only seven when my family built the new home in Romania and do not remember much about the process. What I do remember is that there were stone walls, the trusses were handmade, and the house was covered with tile roofing. Later on I learned that the hay kept in the attic area was a great insulation for the cold days of winter. There was electricity pulled into the new home, but no indoor plumbing nor a ventilation system. Little I knew then, that forty years later I will build my own home at the other end of the world, in the USA.

Building a home is a very exciting experience, however, a major undertaking. I was and continue to be grateful to Garry who was patient with us in explaining how the building process works, about the stages we have to follow, and giving me the opportunity to be his helper in most of the building stages when not contracted out. The learning brought me a new perspective of appreciation toward home building. During the home building process, many of our friends stopped by to see it, help with some work, and give us the assurance that we are doing the right thing. Gary has never had a fixed work schedule and his work hours varied. This allowed me to adjust my DOC work schedule, and be able to be at the work site when he was there. We had our share of barbecued lunches and drinking beer, whenever possible. We are forever grateful to Gary for his work and patience, to Chris for the roofing job, and to Denny and Russ for their help with the landscaping. With Denny and Russ, we started a yearly hunting trip to the Skookum area, a get together that will last over twenty years. Along the way, we included Chris, Joe, and other friends. We still talk about the fun we all had during these trips. Never shot a deer, however, we did not really want to shoot one, we were there for the good times and good times we had.

The new home was ready for us to move in the day after Thanksgiving 1992. There will never be enough words to describe the feelings for this accomplishment! With the help of our friends, we started the move in early in the morning on a crisp cool fall day, and by the finished moving process the ground was covered with a few inches of snow. I was thinking occasionally about how the weather changed in a day from seeing green grass on the ground in the morning and snow in the evening, all in the day we moved into the new family home. Looking in retrospect, I believe that it was a premonition of Almighty, telling us of building the home when relatively young, and living in it to the days of the winter of our lives. As of this time, we lived in our home for more than a quarter of a century and have no plans of moving out. On the contrary, we told our daughter and her children that this home should stay in the family forever, and they promised to do just that.

After moving into our new home, we continued to manage the rental agreements for the house we lived in. Willy was happy with that, as he has not made up his mind on selling the house. As a token of appreciation for the discounted renting price we enjoyed for about six years, we did not charge him for these services. However, we did charge him for the necessary improvements/expenses we incurred with the renters. I remember one time, when calling him on a new charge, he told me that he is more afraid of my call, "than the IRS calling" him. I am sure he said it jokingly.

OUR DAUGHTER'S FIRST WEDDING

Cristina graduated with an LPN degree in 1993 and wanted to move back home, with her boyfriend Marshall. We accepted this arrangement with the condition that they will soon marry. "Living in sin" was something difficult for us to accept, however, we did look at potential consequences if we did not accept it, for a while at least.

As you probably guessed, we were responsible for the wedding cost that after "said and done" amounted to about $16,000. It was a nice ceremony held at the Sacred Heart parish, officiated by our friend Father Joe. The reception was held at one of the reception rooms at the Masonic Temple. We had invited about sixty guests, from our friends' group and Marshall's family and friends. It was actually a lot of fun and everyone enjoyed being there and celebrating with us. Cristina and Marshall enjoyed, or how much Marshall remembered, spending the wedding night at the Honeymoon suite of Coeur d'Alene resort in Idaho.

So, by the end of 1994 while they were married we accepted for them to live with us, while Cristina and Marshall worked as LPNs, with Marshall going to further schooling to get his RN degree. Being responsible only for half of the utilities cost and not having to pay rent, it enabled them to save enough for buying a house a few years later. Life moved on without any serious challenges while Cristina lived with us. Sometimes they wanted to pay even less than their share of the utilities cost, but there wasn't much choice in this matter. Never had any overt argument with Marshall, just long dialogs over various topics, as he was an interesting individual with a very good ability to argue his position on things. A couple of years later, Marshall graduated from the RN program and he asked Neli to "pin him" at the graduation ceremony. This was a token of appreciation toward us helping him out while he went to school.

With all the savings made in a couple of years, Cristina and Marshall bought a beautiful home newly built, in Spokane Valley in the South Century area. The home was not completely finished and between Marshall's stepdad and I, we finished the lower part of the split level home. They bought two German shepherd dogs, so I ended up building a dog house between the garage and the backyard, allowing the dogs to go in and out. It was all good and Trystan and Gavin joined the family shortly after.

DOC DRUG UNIT WORK

Learning how to manage a caseload of law breaking people is not an easy task. People in general, live their life very much in line with the learned experiences, driven by personal ambitions, emotions, and sometimes addictions. Having had numerous interactions with people from different countries and cultures thus far in life, proved to be of great benefit in this line of work.

There were just three CCOs in the Spokane office, tasked with developing a Drug specialized unit: Jack, Debi and I, with Jack being the Lead. We were given caseloads exclusively of Drug offenders having to serve supervision according to the sentence given. Those days, supervision was synonymous with monitoring as treatment and rehabilitation did not carry a lot of emphasis. Drug offenders, generally speaking, have to fight a very serious "demon" and it was not uncommon to make up to three arrests a day. The addiction seems to be so very powerful, that only the next fix matters, and nothing else. We have seen many lives and families destroyed because of it, and oftentimes this is the platform of committing new law violations taking people in a spiral down to the "bottom". There was a young man of twenty-four years of age, who always came to the office to report, walking with a cane, claiming serious back problems and stating he was in great pain. During a field visit in the evening, spotted him in the community with a girlfriend holding hands, appearing to be just fine. Called him to report the next day, and took him to a testing facility for a urinalysis testing. Claiming that he "can't pee", I waited with him there for over four hours, when the facility was just about to close for the day. Given the choice for going to jail for refusing to give a UA or give one and go home, he chose the latter. The next day in the morning, I got a call from a homicide detective, asking me if I had this individual on my caseload. When I said that I do, he said that I did and he was found dead at his home as a result of an apparent overdose. As in all suspicious deaths, an autopsy was scheduled and I was invited to attend. That was not a good decision and here is why: Seeing his body dissected by the Coroner taking different organ samples, I came to realize that I caused this individual demise by the pressure I put on him, driving him to take more drugs because of his fear of incarceration. That guilt, perhaps not realistic, stayed with me for a long time. Those days, with no counseling available to staff with similar experiences, we learned to tough it out.

Law enforcement agencies, and other Drug units across the state, were our close partners. We met regularly and learned from each other how to best do our job without getting hurt. Collaborating with other professionals helped me learn faster, and I got pretty good at what I was doing. Many years down the road, there were a couple of young female drug offenders that I supervised, who came back to let me know how they rebuilt their lives by going to school and getting professional jobs. With their agreement, I enrolled them as DOC volunteers and they assisted me at parenting programs, family events, and celebrations for the offenders and their families. What a wonderful way of modeling a life change. We showed others that change is possible when we want it, and are willing to make sacrifices. There was another lady, whom I did not remember, that came by my office to let me know how successful she became, after she finished her supervision with me. Retired from a successful business, she was a self-made millionaire and a published author of a biography describing her fight with addiction and the recovery process. Later on, when Trystan was twenty years of age, I took him with me to the Refuse/Recycle facility to get rid of the accumulated unwanted things. By the exit booth we had to weigh our truck again and pay the fee. The attendant asked me for my driver's license, then he asked if I remembered him. At first, I did not, but when he said that I supervised and helped him out with strengthening his life thirty years ago, I did remember him. He used to report to the office with his Native American G-friend, who always showed to be a great support to him. He praised me for the help and consideration given when he was in need, and he said that he has never forgotten me. After we left, Trystan said that he was very happy to be with me and witness this testimony about the great work done to help others. I felt good as well, especially with a family member hearing this firsthand.

In the fifth year of working in the Drug unit, I was selected to represent DOC at Spokane County Superior court, Drug court. It was a great honor to be part of a multi-agency team of professionals working with drug offenders who opted to participate in the intensive drug programs, with a chance to avoid conviction when the program was successfully completed. This different program was the first one implemented in Washington state and Judge Jim was the first judge presiding. We had some success stories and we had some failures, just like with any other program. For the most part it was fun, learned a lot, and became a better professional. My interactions with drug offenders exclusively lasted about five years, when I got promoted to a Lead CCO in the Sex Unit.

SUPERVISING SEX OFFENDERS

When promoted to lead the Sex unit of Spokane DOC office, some pundits around the office poked fun at me by saying: "Hey you must have had enough of those drugs, now you moving to sex, and where to next?"

Managing sex offenders living in the community requires a different approach than supervising drug offenders. The dialog with them is carried at a different depth, the network of collateral contacts is by far more extensive, the violation and pre-sentence reports more detailed, and the liability of the supervising officer and the agency when something goes wrong, is much higher. As a lead CCO I was tasked with supervising a specialized L-3 community notification offenders, considered at the highest risk to reoffend. The caseload was much smaller, but the responsibility was much higher. Almost monthly, we had community meetings in conjunction with the Sexual Exploitation unit of Spokane PD, held in the neighborhood where the individual was released. The community was not happy to see a sexual predator moving in, and many questions were asked as to why in my neighborhood?

Worked very close with Detective Jerry, who would become a friend. At these meetings, Jerry would open the meeting by jokingly saying: "I put them in and he lets them out". One can only imagine how eyes were turned to me, and not in a pleasant way. Usually by the end of these meetings, after explaining the legality of our work, most people would understand better but not necessarily accept the upcoming release.

In the Spokane area, we developed an extensive management network, involving most if not all agencies providing services to our offenders and their families: DOC, LE, CPS, Victim advocates, Prosecutor office, Therapists, Polygraph examiners, Landlords, DSHS, etc. Our management work in Spokane was recognized by the National Institute of Justice, and we became a national resource site for other jurisdictions. Stephanie, the prosecutor participating, was the lead of our team and we enjoyed her lead along the years. She was articulate, knowledgeable, and perhaps, ahead of her time with this kind of community involvement. This work involved quite a few trips to other states for sharing information on our supervision strategies in Spokane. No need to say of how much we enjoyed these trips, and the many "unorthodox" things we have done. I liked this aspect of DOC work and learned a great deal about interpersonal communication, multiple facets of the supervision process, and human behavior in general. Recognized for my contributions, I was selected as the CCO of the year for Eastern Region. Did this work for about five years, until 2000.

GRANDCHILDREN JOIN THE FAMILY

Still worked in the Sex unit on St. Patrick's Day of 2000. Cristina went to the hospital early morning for her first child anticipated delivery, and I went to work as I had a community meeting at Spokane Community College. It was a panel discussion of our Sex Offender Management Team with the body of SCC staff, about sex offender management in Spokane. In the middle of the meeting, two of the CCOs in my sex unit entered the conference room dressed in their field attire (body armor, DOC badges displayed along with their side weapons), walking slowly toward the panel where I was seated. All of a sudden, the room got quiet as they came toward me, anticipating perhaps that I would be taken away. They whispered to me that my grandson was born and turned around leaving the area. Overwhelmed by the news, I stood up and shared the message with the still quiet audience. It was a matter of seconds before everyone in the room stood up, applauding for the newcomer. So, our first grandchild Trystan had a welcoming to this world by a body of educators, and St. Patrick's Day became the family favorite holiday for us. A year later, a week before the Memorial Day on May 21st, Gavin became part of the family. As grandparents, at forty-eight and forty-six, we were able to enjoy spending time with our G-kids and live our professional lives at the same time. Life was wonderful!

PARENT'S ROLE EXPANDS

My wife and I enjoyed assuming the G-parents role and spent most of our free time providing care for Trystan and Gavin. Starting with babysitting, reading bedtime stories, taking them for stroll rides in our neighborhood and the local parks, building them a playground place, were new things to do that brought a new dimension to our lives. Cristina and Marshall were working full time with a fixed schedule, therefore Neli and I adjusted our work schedule to meet the childcare demands. It was not easy as we had to meet our own job requirements, but somehow we made it work for the sake of keeping the family together.

Keeping the family together is the job of all, and when some are out of sync, is like driving a car with a flat tire. Making a number of poor decisions by buying new vehicles and other buyings on credit, brought Cristina and Marshall to the point of having to deal with an overly stressed family life. After living together for about five years, their marriage fell apart and the divorce ended with a bankruptcy on top. No need to say how hurt we were when Cristina told us of their decision to separate, and because of the overly involved role we had with caring for Trystan and Gavin made the pain even worse. Marshall left Cristina and their two children in the house, and we had to work things out and move her to our place as the home had to be vacated. As parents, it is difficult to describe how we felt about seeing our daughter having to come back home and live with us, this time with her two children that were two-and-a-half and one-and-a-half.

Again, Almighty gave us strength and understanding that Cristina was twenty-five years old and still had the ability to rebuild her life. To help her out, we bought a fixer upper home for her somewhere in the mid-Valley, on Cataldo. She stayed with us while with the help of my friends we refurbished the house, inside and out, and made it a nice home for her children and her. For us it was a major financial undertaking as we ended up with an expense of over $30,000.00. It was a lot of money spent, but for a good reason and peace of mind that our daughter had a home to live in with her two children. Fate had it differently for us.

.

CRISTINA MOVES ON TO A NEW RELATIONSHIP

While still working at finishing the work at the house we just bought, Cristina has met Jon, who was one of her classmates in HS. He was divorced and apparently Cristina liked the idea of letting him move in with her and their two children. Respecting Cristina's choice, we decided to rent the house to Cristina and Jon, who soon got married in Las Vegas. Paying for their flight there, I was disappointed when I heard that Jon paid for his best friend's flying ticket to accompany them to Las Vegas. It was things like this, and others that I would rather not elaborate about, that made me realize that Cristina moved on with the relationship too fast, but it was her decision not ours.

While still living together, Cristina decided to further her education, from an LPN to an RN level. It was another year of school and we had made the decision to help out with rent forgiveness and a lot of child care for Trystan and Gavin. A year later, Cristina got her RN degree and in 2007 we had a new granddaughter joining the family. Jolene Elena Hall was a delight for us all and the two boys were very kind to her. Cristina was very happy to have her and to earn a better living as an RN.

I built them a playground at their home and they also had one at our house. Every time they came over, depending on the season, we would spend our time playing outside, going for stroll rides, bike rides, and playing games. Silverwood theme park, in Idaho, became our stomping ground. For many years we bought season passes for all to enjoy. Chess was a favorite game for Trystan and Gavin, who were fascinated by the computer battle chess game. Trystan was four when he knew the name of all the chess figures and their place on the chess board. That brought him a chess board cake for his fourth birthday. On his terms, Gavin learned the game also and these days I have difficult times struggling to win a chess game with them. Joline has never shown much interest in the game, however, she knows the game basics and hopes that later on she will learn more. Gavin took on his own to care for fixing bottles for Jolene, making sure she is fed and taken care of. In the winter, I took them for snow tubing rides behind the lawn mower, in the front and the backyard. We would build snowmen and snow caves that delighted them with endless fun. As they grew a bit older, we would make a yearly trip to Silver Mountain for snow tubing. My favorite part was the nap time, when I would read stories, from the books and tell them some from the mythology I was fascinated by when growing up. I was so very glad to see them all liking it, knowing well that it will instill the desire to learn and develop imagination. And the future confirmed the very thing.

MOVING ON WITH DOC WORK

Our grandchildren became the focus of our lives and Neli and I would not do much without them. Occasionally, the work has not remained the focus, but still required its daily demands for both of us. Neli had not had major changes with her line of work, with the exception of the company she worked for changing hands on a couple occasions. With DOC, was a different story.

Shortly after Trystan was born, in the summer of 2000, I was promoted to a Community Corrections Specialist position, and started working for the newly developed Risk Management Unit. I still believe that this was happening as when I was the Lead CCO in the Sex unit: I was part of the implementation process of the Risk management; worked already certain aspects of it; was the Chair of Spokane Sex Offender Management Team; and recognized as the Community Correction Officer of the year. The promotion brought a substantial raise and different role responsibilities: developing release plans to the NE area of our Spokane county for: the L-3 sex offenders (most likely to reoffend); high needs offenders; imminent threat offenders; and violent ones. If the previous work required many interactions with other agencies, this job expanded it by far. Travel to different prisons (twelve in WA) was often and required to meet the offenders before release, assess risk and needs and then follow up with additional phone conferences involving all that are or will be part of case management and support groups. Very busy, but extremely rewarding job as it gave me the ability to be creative, resourceful, help develop my communication and customer service skills, that were of paramount importance in this job.

One day, coming back to Spokane from a trip out of town, I had a unique experience. Merging into I-90 from 395 S. into Ritzville, I drove through the foot of a rainbow. Pulled over and just marveled at the unique spectrum of hundreds of colors the water droplets had. I felt surrounded with feelings of hope for the future, going through such experience. Rainbows, while uplifting to look at because of the majestic view they offer, seem to be elusive to most of us. So, this unique experience went right next to being blessed by the Pope experience I had in Rome, Italy. Almighty again?

Oftentimes the change of DOC Secretary, brings operational and legislative changes, liked and welcomed by staff, or the opposite. For unknown reasons, this Secretary decided to terminate the Risk management process that worked very well for about ten years. Apparently with the intent to engage every staff in the re-entry process, he chose to eliminate the team of about thirty staff that were working this exclusively. It was a false premise, did not work as intended and still does not, ten years later.

Being state employees and governed by the state Merit rules, staff on our team was transferred to other positions as available and dictated by seniority. At the time, I had two choices: transfer to the Marshall coordinated Fugitive team with other 2 DOC staff (apprehending fugitives on warrant status), or assume the same level position with the Family Services Unit. Both positions would require additional training for the job duties: for the Fugitive unit, BLEA (Basic Law Enforcement Academy), and for the Family Services, Facilitator and customer service training. Working as a CCO and CCS for twenty years, I was very familiar with the Law Enforcement demands of the job, and at the same time, I was fully aware that I would be under a serious learning curve with the facilitating training/work of the other.

Mulling over this with a high stress level, I chose the latter and replaced the existing Family Specialist in the Family Services Unit (FSU), with less seniority. Starting a new thing in the traditional DOC line of work is never easy, just like starting all other things in life. However, I was determined to do it, and in no time my life experience, and DOC experience and training helped me not only do it well, but exceeded my own and others' expectations. Our team of four, with previous work engagements/relationships, was working well and got recognized for "Going the extra mile" at the Agency and the Governor's levels. Not working directly with incarcerated or on supervision offenders, eliminated that "not being too successful with the work done" feeling. Helping families left behind navigate the correctional system, solve conflicts at the lowest resolution level, teaching parenting programs to offenders and their families, and providing customer service as the first contact families have with DOC, brings in a different sense of accomplishment. I would even say enthusiasm, to a job not usually much appreciated by the community at large. I do like it well, and hope to coast into retirement from it.

New Developments at Home

We loved our G-kids and we did all we could to offer them what we did not have growing up. Right or wrong, we decided to go this way with keeping in mind that our g-kids have by far more than we did, but they have to learn about life during the growing up years. As G-parents, we pledged "a dollar a day" until their eighteenth B-days. From their young ages, we started to put a lot of emphasis on school work, good behavior, and taking care of their health. Somehow, through numerous repetitive practices, they seem to have learned this. What helped the most, I believe, is that we modeled what we tried to teach them.

With Gary again, we built a 24'x48' detached building that we divided in four segments: storage; gym, wine room and sauna. In this building that we called the "fun room" we did lots of things together: learned how to play ping-pong, shooting hoops, air hockey, shooting BB guns and learning the gun rules, etc. The gun rules are universal and learning early in life, proved to be very useful when we ended up buying firearms for Cristina, Trystan and Gavin and went target shooting. All of them, including Jolene, observed these rules and they made it easy when we did it. What a wonderful gift, both ways.

The wine room was for me to learn something I was always intrigued by: how to make my own wine and have a place dedicated to do it. Started a couple of years before in the garage attached to the house. Experimented with some country wine (made of fruits) and it seemed to be good. I remember an occurrence when during the transfer process (from Carboy to Carboy – five gallons glass bottle) while keeping tasting I liked it, and brought out some cheese to enhance the taste buds. Next thing I knew, I woke up on the couch inside the house and the garage floor had wine all over spilling from the carboys. So, I put this in my experience toolbag, and built a room dedicated to it. From then on, I experimented with making Merlot, Syrah, and a variety of county wines. We have been blessed with plenty of plums from our plum trees, blackberries from our blackberry bushes, pears from our pear trees, red and black currants from our bushes, and plenty of cherries from our cherry tree. Of course I ended up giving a lot away to friends and for some charities at work, but I did not make many trips to the liquor store after this. I still consider this hobby as the most rewarding one an individual can have. So, after more than half a century when I lived next door to a winery, I became the Vintner of my own.

In 2012, we decided to enhance what we already had, and built an inground swimming pool (16'x32'), with an automatic cover. Quite an experience (expensive one might say), that we enjoyed greatly and the memories it brought us are never going to be forgotten. Our G-kids were delighted with the diving board, slide, and the volleyball net. We still enjoy it and thus, expanded our work out, and brought a taste of the "sea shore" to our backyard.

So, life was good and we enjoyed our numerous interactions with our G-kids. Jon was part of the family and he was not. I will expound on that. Somehow, he continued to express many disagreements with Cristina and later with Trystan and Gavin. There were a few episodes where Cristina asked him to leave the house because of his behavior. Most of the time this happened, he would call or email me and wanted to disclaim himself from doing anything wrong. When meeting with him, always emphasized the importance of working out the differences and keeping the family together. In a way, I did see that he felt as not being in control of his affairs as he was renting the home from us and/or some other reasons. Understanding that, without my wife's full consent, we went ahead and signed over the house to them for what the mortgage was at the time. With all improvements made to the house, the equity built was over $30,000.00. Their immediate plan after that was to sell the house and move into a bigger and better place. Nothing wrong with that, but we were asked to allow them to live with us for "a while", saving some money for the new purchase. We agreed and that proved to be a big mistake.

So, fate had it again: He got in a verbal conflict with Trystan and Cristina asked him to leave our house. We continued to provide for Cristina and her children while Jon lived with his parents. Unbeknown to us, they kept in communication and found a new home to move in. While it was good to see them together again, we did not like the way they did it. With the equity money from the sale of the house on Cataldo, they ended up buying a home in the Northwood area and moved in, taking all belongings stored at our house.

Did not talk much with them for a while, mainly because we were hurt. On top of that, we decided to have Neli's teeth taken care of and went with the implant approach. It was a long and expensive venture, but one of the best decisions we have made for her to grow old with dignity. The dental surgeon, Dr. Higuchi, offered her a considerable discount by having her participate in a new experimental implant process. My Neli was so very brave going through painful surgeries and bone graft processes. As always, the end result matters, and now she enjoys her healthy mouth.

As almost always, if things are not aggravated they will work out in the long run. We kept to ourselves and hoped for the best. Shortly after, we started visiting Cristina and Jon at the new home and we developed a new standard of normal. The home was very spacious, well put together, the G-kids had their own bedrooms, and it looked nice. The outside yard work/landscape needed some dire improvements, but if they did not take action, we would not offer assistance.

CRISTINA'S SECOND DIVORCE

If we pay attention to details and small occurrences in our lives, we can almost foresee the future. The relationship between Cristina and Jon started deteriorating and with one more anger burst, he was asked to leave the house. The divorce was imminent and expensive, but Cristina seemed to have decided to part ways with Jon after ten years of marriage.

With that said, I don't want anyone to believe that Cristina was not part of the conflict. With her over spending inclinations, one can say that she aggravated the matter some. But she has always been a good mother and took good care of her kids, a thing we always appreciated greatly.

In June 2017, we took Cristina and her children on a ten-day vacation to Washington D.C. It was an event none of us will be forgetting. Walking daily, from landmark to landmark, they had the opportunity to see and learn about the American history. What a wonderful gift to our child and G-kids!

The divorce was painful for us all, Jon included. We had a talk with Cristina and she agreed to follow a three-year plan we laid out for her to fully recover, financially and at her own pace, emotionally. As of now, she has stayed with the recovery plan, is doing very well, made quite a few improvements to her home and takes great care of her children who are happy and developing well. In a two-year time, her home got a new gutter system, a backyard cedar fence, a 10'x10' storage shed, two dogs (Bela and Kylo) with a dog house, six new trees for the backyard and one in the front, a 200-square-foot cedar deck, a hot tub, and a gas fire pit on the deck.

With Gary again, we finished her home attic, a spacious 700 square feet, where Trystan has moved in on his eighteenth B-day.

Trystan graduated HS in 2018, and Gavin in 2019. Both were enrolled in the EWU Running start program, while in their senior year. Jolene started middle school in 2018. What a wonderful accomplishment while applying ongoing teachings: do well in school, behave, and take care of your health. They were both rewarded with a new car when turning eighteen years of age and further supported by us all, while meeting the three mandatory requirements.

As mentioned earlier, on his eighteenth B-day Trystan moved into his new living arrangements, but not alone. His HS sweetheart moved in with him. This was a relationship of over three years that culminated with their decision to live together, now that the space was available. Sometimes these living arrangements don't work out, and in their case, they did not. Greatly affected by the unexpected outcome, Trystan experienced some high levels of anxiety and was at the loss. We had a heart to heart talk about available emotional recovery options, with him choosing to go on a two-month vacation in Romania. With Alin's help, he enjoyed seeing the country's attractions, my hometown, and the extended family. We believe, and he agreed, that the visit to Romania helped a great deal with healing the emotional scars of the lost relationship. He is the first from my G-kids that had a chance to see my growing up "stomping ground". He was also the last one to interact with my nephew Alin, who passed away in 2020.

Training as an athlete, shortly after turning eighteen years of age, Gavin completed the Half Iron Man seventy-five-mile race in Coeur D'Alene, Idaho. He was the youngest competitor in the race and we all were so very proud of him and his will power. In 2020, Gavin and Kennedy, his beautiful G-friend, built their own RV with the floor plan of their choice, and before winter they went on a ten-day vacation in Utah. What a resourceful team!

The COVID-19 pandemic came upon us sometime in March 2020, as it did with the rest of the world. We are fortunate to be able to continue with our work, including Trystan and Gavin, who put school on hold until classes resume in person. Jolene continued with the distance learning, and moved in with us, taking the bedroom and day room downstairs. One day, Neli went downstairs to look around and see if Jolene had all that she needed. To her surprise, Neli found all the ingredients needed for a makeshift inhaling station, dirty dishes under the bed, etc. Immediately,

Cristina decided to take Jolene to her dad for a while, giving her time to think on what she has done wrong. It must have affected Jolene a great deal, as she chose not to speak with us for a few months and not call us until Christmas, after she got her presents. She continues to live at her Dad's house during the pandemic. Recently, she resumed coming over to dinner and even spending the night with us. We have never lost hope that someday soon, Jolene will follow her brothers' footsteps, and she will resume being a delight to us all. We love her dearly!

As of now Neli, Gavin, and myself, tested positive of COVID-19, fortunately with no significant symptoms. Neli and Cristina got vaccinated, I got my first shot of the vaccine on February 4 and the second one coming up on March 4, 2021.

Neli has retired from her work in May 2020, however, continues with on-call work whenever she decides to take it.

I continue with my work at WA DOC, and hope to be able to retire on my seventieth B-day, October 2022.

Merging Lives and the American Dream

The initial intent for this writing was for Cristina and her children to learn about their roots, their heritage, the ongoing struggles and hard work involved while we reached sustainability and happiness in America, our newfound home country for thirty-nine years now. In this process, since we left our home country (Romania), we spent a year in a refugee camp, finished higher education, built a new home, and held professional jobs. Our lives merged with many other wonderful people's lives, and this helped and inspired us along the way.

Living in the best country in the world, our lives converged with many other people's lives, leading to achieving the American dream. It was hard work with many sacrifices, and continues to be an ongoing work to keep the dream many people in the world wish to reach: the American dream.

Being blessed to see our child reaching self-sufficiency as a consummate Health professional, enjoying our G-kids to their way to maturity and doing well, and Neli and I enjoying a good health growing old, is the best gift from Almighty, and for that we will ever be grateful.

REFERENCES/SOURCES

1. Fisher, Stephen G., Romania, New York: Praeger Publications, 1957
2. Keefee, Eugene K., et al, Romania A Country Study, Washington, D.C.: The American University, 1979
3. Nelan, Bruce W., "Unfinished Revolution," Time, No. 01, (January 1990)
4. Radea, Mihori, "The price of Liberty in Romania, "Mirco-Magazine, No. 04, December 1989
5. Radea, Mihori, "A Strange Government," Micro-Magazine, No. 3, January 1990

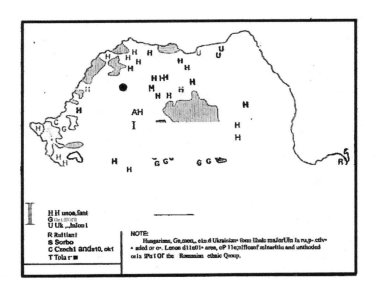

Source: Adapted !rom Ian M: Matley, Romania: A profile, New York, 1970, p. 276

Figure 3 Romania, Distribution of Ethnic Group, 1966